D1015702

MAN
THE FALLEN
APE

Branko Bokun

Doubleday & Company, Inc.
Garden City, New York
1977

Library of Congress Cataloging in Publication Data

Bokun, Branko, 1920–
  Man: the fallen ape.

  Bibliography: p. 206.
  1. Social evolution.   2. Human evolution.
3. Psychology, Comparative.   4. Civilization, Ancient.
5. Women—History.   I. Title.
GN360.B64   301.2
ISBN 0-385-11629-2
Library of Congress Catalog Card Number 76-18335

Acknowledgments

I would like to acknowledge the co-operation and assistance of Dr. Petar Bokun, head of the Psychiatric Hospital in Split, who tested many of the theories in this book against his own research, and who served as collaborator and confidant throughout the writing of this book.

I would also like to thank Mrs. John Loudon and Mrs. Marina Cobbold for their research and collaboration.

Contents

Author's Note

Before starting this book I would like to explain the meaning of certain words which might otherwise be associated with different concepts, thereby causing misunderstanding.

As, in my view, men and women had two separate evolutions, the term "man" will refer to the human male and not to mankind as a whole.

The term "opportunism" will be intended as the practice of taking the best advantage of objective circumstances in any given moment, with no regard for principles or ultimate consequences.

The word "brain" will mean the organ of thought. "Intelligence" will mean the understanding of nature and its laws. The "mind" will mean the brain's special faculty of creating abstract, supernatural, or transcendental ideas.

Homo sapiens will mean man with a developed mind, capable of abstract thinking.

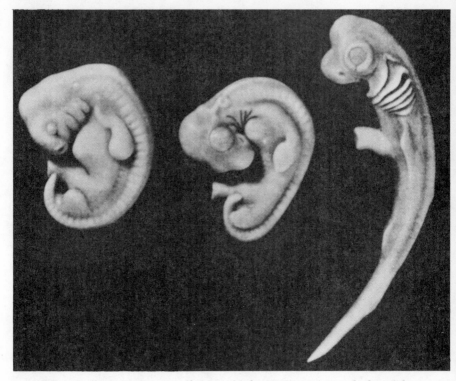

The similarity of man (left), chicken (center), and dog-fish (right) in their embryo stage.

PART ONE

The Origin of the Human Species

For years I pondered on what an ape's account of the history of mankind would be like. An animal is necessarily closer to nature —its laws and its logic—than a human. Only a being whose logic has not been influenced by its mind could explain the history of mankind without prejudice.

Acquiring the mind, humans lost their natural logic, which means that their explanation of natural phenomena, particularly their own existence, cannot but be biased. They also like to explore the known with the unknown.

The ape could begin his history of mankind with modern mankind, whose latest product contains each step of its own evolution. It is unnecessary to speculate about the meaning of fossils. All fossils of the human species can be found in any living human being. Human abstract thoughts are the results of the brain, a brain programed by the major events in the life of the human species. However proud of our mind we may be, the mind cannot create *ex nihilo*. By analyzing abstract human creations we can uncover the major happenings in the evolution of the human species, the happenings which have conditioned or inspired these abstract creations.

It is useless to study wild animals in order to understand humans, because they have little in common as far as their behavior is concerned. Most animals are naturally complete beings possessing some innate pattern of behavior, hereditarily transmitted. Their specialization, the result of an evolution which helps them to find harmony with the universe and its laws, is evidence of their completeness, their correct place in nature, their best way in given circumstances of surviving and reproducing. In brief, they have realized a stable relationship between their specialization and their environment.

Humans are incomplete beings. Lacking specialization, they are open to change with any change of circumstance. The human animal, in contrast to other animals, is unpredictable. Animals inherit their pattern of behavior; humans have to learn it.

It is also pointless to study animals in captivity in order to understand mankind. Animals in unnatural surroundings behave unnaturally.

Furthermore it is fruitless to compare our human ancestors with present-day aborigines or Bushmen. There is far more of our ancestors in modern "civilized" mankind, particularly when confronted with fear or great anxiety in exlex situations, than in so-called modern "primitive" mankind. Besides, the modern primitives have a culture, often a very homogeneous culture, and a mind with the capacity for creating abstract thoughts, neither of which our ancestors possessed before Homo sapiens.

The study of prehistory, working backward from modern man, could be even more dangerous, however, than research through fossils or through other animals. Scientists will always uncover what suits their beliefs, prejudices, metaphysical preconceptions, or simply their conceit. A convinced Marxist will find that prehistoric society was based on the collective possession of the means and tools of production. A capitalist will discover, by analogy to other animals' behavior patterns, that private domain or the "territorial imperative" were more important to man than the sexual drive, because without the former, mating was impossible.

An example of how human logic can differ can be seen in the disputes between the East and West concerning the Russian opponents of the Soviet regime. Many dissidents went to lunatic asylums and were treated as mentally sick. Western doctors and the press accused Soviet doctors of being blind instruments of the regime and of having broken the solemn oath of their calling. The Russian doctors thought the West had gone mad in reproaching their behavior. For them, anyone who opposed such an efficient police power must be mentally disturbed. In their view, only those who had what Seneca called *Libido morienti* (the death wish) would dare to provoke the State. The Russian doctors were convinced that they were undertaking a humanitarian mission by placing the opponents of the regime in asylums and thereby reducing their aggression—the only hope for their survival. To reduce the outstanding to mediocrity was always a medical and human duty in a state where mediocrity had the better chance of survival.

In Western countries, proud of their Christian civilization, anyone imitating Christ's advice of "If thou wilt be perfect, go and sell that that thou hast, and give to the poor," would either be locked up or imprisoned for impersonating Christ. Yet it is quite natural for Christians to believe in miracles and the supernatural.

When Darwin published his thesis, the majority of humanity considered his opponents logical when they protested: "It is better to have a God as a father, than an ape."

Another reason why research in the origin of mankind cannot be carried out objectively by humans is because humans glorify their ancestors and their origin. Perhaps this is why authors such as Robert Ardrey, Jacob Bronowski, Konrad Lorenz, and Desmond Morris are so appealing.

Idealistic philosophy has influenced mankind to glorify itself and its ancestors. Reading some of the books on the origin of mankind, one receives the impression that our ancestors separated from the apes and faced the vicissitudes of the savannah merely to please the ego of modern man and give him the illusion of superiority.

Konrad Lorenz, in his book *On Aggression* stressed the following apologetic words: ". . . and who has gained insight into evolution, will be able to apprehend the unique position of man. We are the highest achievement reached so far by the great constructors of evolution." Seven pages later Lorenz writes: "Unreasoning and unreasonable human-nature causes two nations to compete, though no economic necessity compels them to do so; it induces two political parties or religions with amazingly similar programmes of salvation, to fight each other bitterly and impels an Alexander or Napoleon to sacrifice millions of lives in his attempt to unite the world under his sceptre" . . . "and we are so accustomed to the phenomena that most of us fail to realise how abjectly stupid and undesirable the historical mass behaviour of humanity actually is."

The genius of Darwin has its moments of adolescent infatuation. "The world," he writes, "it has often been remarked, appears as if it had long been preparing for the advent of man: and this in one sense is strictly true for he owes his birth to a long line of progenitors." But many animals have just as long a line of progenitors as humans, most even longer. Darwin should have known that even Caesar who, in the agony of death, adjusted his toga to cover his nudity, or the stoic death of Antoninus Pius, are nothing in comparison with the greatness implicit in the behavior of dog described by Darwin himself in his book *The Descent of Man:* ". . . and everyone has heard of the dog suffering under vivisection, who licked the hand of the operator."

Some scientists, such as Lévy-Bruhl, call the mental activity of humanity following the advent of Homo sapiens "logical," and the mental activity preceding Homo sapiens, "pre-logical." In my view, ever since man discovered his brain and the mind's power to create abstract thoughts, he entered an era of beliefs, an era in which he remains today. "Homo" is more *credulus* than *sapiens.* In this era of beliefs man is consequent to his beliefs, to his prejudices and to his abstract convictions. This is contrary to logic. It is the logic of a believer, but not of a rational being. The human female can be logical, but we live in a man's world, a supernatural world, a world created by man's mind, a world which rejects a natural intelligence and its logic. Man's abstract world is man's refuge from reality. Any believer finds it quite logical to obey, without question, the orders of his superiors.

In this book I will do my utmost to detach myself as far as possible from human logic in favor of natural logic and to interpret mankind's past and present more objectively. Many theories on the origin of mankind and its evolution have been nothing but pure and often naïve speculations. "Most books concerning the

MAN: THE FALLEN APE

origin of humans," Ellen Morgan explains in her *The Descent of Woman* "include some phrases such as 'the early stages of man's evolutionary progress remain a total mystery.' " The following statement of Sherwood L. Washbourne confirms my view. "The study of human evolution is a game rather than a science in the usual sense." At a meeting in London in 1975 of fossil man experts, F. C. Howell said: "We ought to throw away a lot of ideas and try to start anew."

Scientists today explain that mankind came from the killer-ape who separated from his non-aggressive cousin and advanced his status because of his predatory life. In order to hunt he became upright and by using his hands he developed his brain.

There are many people who still believe that humanity was created by God. According to Archbishop Usher's "Kallender," God created mankind on March 23, 4004 B.C. In propounding this date the Archbishop ignored the fact that the Egyptians already had a real calendar in 4241 B.C.

The main difference of opinion on the origin of mankind lies between paleontologists and serologists. The former claim that the separation of humans from apes occurred between 15 and 50 million years ago, the exact date varying from author to author; whereas the serologists, led by Vincent Sarich, an American molecular biologist, explain that the separation of man from ape occurred only 4 million years ago.

I will start with the presupposition that one can see in the final product both its origin and its stages of evolution.

Mankind is a singular species in nature with a number of unique peculiarities. Logically, therefore, the history of humanity should be a history of these peculiarities. It is also logical that a unique end-product must have had a unique beginning.

From the very beginning our ancestors must have been more open to development than other animal species. What kind of animal can be open to development? Surely only an underdeveloped animal. The human species must have started from a state of inferiority, a unique inferiority.

Darwin proclaims that *Natura non fecit saltum* (Nature does not jump). This is true, but nature can create abnormalities, not by jumping forward but by slipping behind, by halting at an earlier stage of development.

THE ORIGIN OF THE HUMAN SPECIES 5

The main peculiarity is that humans are ready to perform sexual intercourse at any time, while other animals are only sexually aroused during the so-called mating season, or at the time of oestrus. What is more, humans are the only species to organize their lives around sexual pleasure.

In order to understand what really happened at the beginning we must point out another peculiarity of mankind. Human beings are the only species of animal lacking the instinct to reproduce. Humans reproduce by accident as a result of sexual pleasure.

Lack of an instinct for reproduction caused lack of an instinct for preservation of the species. Lack of an instinct for preservation of the species explains the ease with which humans destroy each other, their indifference to the future of mankind.

The amount of contraceptives used and the number of abortions performed underlines this. Mankind, however conceited or proud it is, must admit that behind the origin of every human being there is no noble instinct of reproduction or any generous feeling toward the species, but merely sensual pleasure sometimes in a drunken or drugged state, a pleasure often obtained by money, deceit, or rape.

It is impossible to imagine the number of people walking the streets of this world whose conception was unwanted, but whose foetal life was not terminated because of some religious, legal, or moral prejudice, or through financial straits. Most accidentally pregnant women would laugh at the poetic thought of Novalis, who saw in every child an *amour devenu visible*.

Before starting to explain the origin of these human peculiarities, it is necessary to explain briefly what happened before mankind came into existence.

Scientists estimate the creation of the earth at about 4,500 million years ago. Approximately 4,000 million years ago the sea was formed; 500 million years later the first life appeared in the water in the form of single-celled algae and bacteria. Though there are several theories about the origin of life, only one thing is positive: life, once started, being life, started breeding life. Organisms evolved from other organisms following the elementary law of life: the survival of a better biological adaptation. *"Le rêve de*

MAN: THE FALLEN APE

toute cellule vivante est de devenir deux cellules," wrote François Jacob.

We can calculate the appearance of the first oxygen-breathing animals at approximately 900 million years ago, and the development of various species of fish at 400–600 million years ago; 430 million years ago land plants began to grow. Between 300–400 million years ago the amphibians, reptiles, and insects started to evolve. Approximately 230 million years ago the dinosaurs appeared, followed by mammals and, some 30 million years later, birds.

Around 70–75 million years ago, the ancestors of our ancestors, small, ratlike insectivores, left their perilous life on ground level for a safer one in the trees. In these small, tree-shrew type of mammals who chose an arboreal environment for reasons of safety, is the origin of the primate. The first page of the history of mankind opens in the woodlands of East Africa.

Most scientists calculate the appearance of monkeys and apes to be about 40 million years ago. They explain that the oldest manlike primate, Ramapithecus, lived in Africa and India about 10 million years ago. Australopithecus lived in Africa approximately 1½ million years ago and is considered to be our direct ancestor. Approximately one million years ago we meet so-called *Homo habilis,* the tool user or tool-maker, and at the same time humans started walking upright. About 130,000 years ago Neanderthal people were in North Africa and Europe, but 20,000 years ago they dwindled with the appearance of Homo sapiens.

This is a general picture of the evolution of mankind until the arrival of Homo sapiens, as presented by most scientists today.

Desmond Morris in *The Naked Ape* describes this important era in the following two phrases: "The ancestors of the only other surviving ape—the naked ape—struck out, left the forest, and threw themselves into competition with the already efficiently adapted ground dwellers. It was a risky business but in terms of evolutionary success it paid dividends"—a statement which sounds more like a financial report than a statement of history.

Carlton S. Coon, in his book *The History of Man,* compresses the most vital events in mankind's past into the following three sentences: "From some kind of a Miocene ape probably living in

Africa, both living apes and men are descended. The apes' ancestors, after a trial period on the ground, swung back into the trees. Ours stayed below, rose onto their hind-legs, made tools, walked, talked and became hunters."

In other words, humans and apes decided one day to come down from the trees, to leave an environment ideal from the point of view of food and security. Then the apes, the less advanced animals, returned to the trees and lived happily ever after, while the more advanced humans walked out of their natural paradise into the hell of the savannah.

In the savannah the human ancestors, with no natural specialization, small and fragile (about 2½ feet tall), with a brain not more than a third of the size of the gorilla today (i.e. one seventh the capacity of that of modern man), had to live and compete with highly specialized and dangerous predators. In natural logic, our human ancestors could only have made this step if they were urged on by a strange desire to commit collective suicide. We must remember that originally the ancestors of primates fled from the dangerous ground into the safety of the trees, a wise step which must have left a trace on their brain. No animal will ever leave a safe environment for a dangerous one, especially when it has an inbuilt and atavistic fear of the danger. This atavistic fear of falling is occasionally experienced in our nightmares.

Scientists do not explain why our human ancestors separated from the apes' ancestors and initiated their own evolution. Nor have they ever explained what the anomaly was which affected our ancestors and launched the human species, an anomaly which must have been present from the start, and one on which depends our separation from the other apes, and our uniqueness.

What follows is my explanation of the beginning of the human species.

In the Eocene epoch (36–58 million years ago) there was already a distinction between the anthropoids and the prosimians. The former were humanlike primates, the latter included ancestors of lemurs, tarsiers, and tree shrews.

Our ancestors lived in company with the ancestors of apes. The law of natural and sexual selection was in operation. From their former existence as lower mammals, the primates inherited a hierarchical system of organization. In this oriental type of male tyranny we find polygamy. In this hierarchical society the female assumes the rank of the male she is copulating with, her aim being to copulate with the highest rank possible. Primates only copulate when the female is in heat. During this period the female develops a distinct odor which arouses the instinct of reproduction in the males. This was the system which human ancestors and ape ancestors respected.

Before continuing, I must clear up an important point. Scientists, ever since Spencer and Darwin, have talked of the "struggle of life," the "survival of the fittest" and "sexual selection," but none explain exactly what is meant by the "fittest." Does it mean the strongest physically—or the most intelligent—in subjugating the other males? My belief is that in the fight for pre-eminence within the highest rank in the group, it was not the cleverest or most intelligent who won. It was not even the strongest physically, although strength often coincides with fitness. In the animal world the individual with the strongest fighting spirit, with the most determination, will impose himself on the others. But what dictates the fighting spirit in a male? It must be the level of maturity in his instinct for reproduction—the main instinct in nature, stronger than the instinct of survival—survival serving the former.

This will be clearer by citing a relevant fact. When one reads that in the struggle for sex and for survival it is the fittest who wins, one immediately has an impression of war, a *bellum omnium contra omnes*, a fight to the death inter-species and intra-species. It has even been called a "jungle law," or simply a "jungle." But in a jungle there is no "jungle." Even in relations between predator and prey there is order. Between predator and prey there is no hatred or unnecessary killing. The struggle in the jungle is very civilized in comparison with human struggles. In the jungle, and particularly between males of the same species, we see more a display of strength than a use of it. In this display it is not the fittest who wins—victory presupposes a fight—which is not logical in nature. In a display of strength (more correctly described as a display of determination to fight if necessary), it is not the more determined who wins; it is the less determined to fight who concedes the victory. Nature survives through an elementary law that the less fit acknowledges the fitter, paying homage to him and either abiding by his order, or withdrawing from the group. Flight is the rule in nature. Fight is the exception which occurs when the flight of the less fit is impossible.

On the fringes of any group of human and ape ancestors there was always a group of omega males. These individuals were there because their instinct for reproduction was not mature enough to compete; it had ceased to develop at an earlier stage. Competition is not a facet of a weak instinct for reproduction. This observation must have induced humans—aeons later—to tame animals by castration. These omega bachelors were biologically adult, able to copulate and procreate, but their instinct for reproduction was not strong enough to urge them to compete for sex with other males. In an abulic state, they followed the group at a distance, indulging from time to time in illegal intercourse with an undisciplined or randy female. It is to these omega ape individuals we may look for our first ancestors. Humans have one pair of chromosomes less than gorillas and chimpanzees.

Had their illegal copulation not resulted in offspring, they would have died out without leaving a trace. The male offspring of this unnatural copulation, if inheriting his father's slow-maturing instinct for reproduction, would join the omega individuals. If, however, he felt a strong instinct he would join the group in search of a rank. The female offspring who inherited the father's low instinct for reproduction started the history of a new species: mankind. This female, with underdeveloped oestrus due to the immaturity of her instinct for reproduction would, on reaching adulthood, start to solicit the hierarchy in search of copulation. In her soliciting of the males, she was not urged on by the instinct for reproduction but by another instinct developing in underdeveloped beings—the instinct of imitation. Imitation of the superior, of the grown-up, is increased by feelings of insufficiency, by an internal itch of the immature, by the frustration of the underdeveloped. Soliciting without oestrus, without the scent to provoke sexual reaction in the males, was soon considered by the hierarchy to be contrary to natural order, and abnormality and a nuisance to the males. In nature, order rejects disorder. This abnormal female ape, soliciting in imitation but

MAN: THE FALLEN APE

without oestrus, was soon chased out of the group. There, on its fringes, she joined the omega bachelors.

These insufficient omega individuals had one positive quality. They were receptive to any new development, any new life. Animal trainers are well aware that it is easier to train an omega individual than an individual of a superior rank.

Soon the new females seduced the omega bachelors.

"The male monkey cannot in fact mate with the female without her invitation and her willingness to co-operate," Leonard Williams states in *Man and Monkey*.

These omega males performed intercourse by imitation. Because of the lack of the odor of oestrus of the new females, their sexual participation was unnatural. There were no natural means or methods of sexual attraction between our ancestors. Today there are none either.

Soon our human ancestors felt pleasure in the imitation of mating, that unique pleasure that only humans, these inferior beings, can experience, the pleasure of achievement—the excitement of performing an act reserved for superior beings. For other animals mating was the normal course of nature.

Slowly mankind became an imitating species. Imitation became the human specialization. Humans learned to run, swim, jump, food-gather, hunt, and fish, all by imitating the specializations of other animals. "No animal voluntarily imitates an action performed by man," Darwin says. Why, indeed, should animals imitate humans, when human actions are a bad imitation of their own? How clumsy we must seem to fish when we swim, or to predators when we run or hunt.

Imitation is the activity of an incomplete being in search of completeness. Successful imitation results in orgasmic pleasure. Orgasmic pleasure is the feeling of achievement experienced by an incomplete being. Only humans can attain orgasmic pleasure, and only through successful imitation, not only in sexual acts but in any other imitative performance. People who are overly self-confident or who, under the sway of some abstract belief, consider themselves complete beings, such as saints or mystics, are not interested in sex.

Man, being more incomplete than woman, experiences more orgasmic pleasures. One example of male orgasmic pleasure can be seen when members of a football team hug and kiss each other after one of their team has scored a goal.

That orgasm is the result of successful imitation can be proved by post-orgasmic exhaustion. Imitation requires an effort—successful imitation even more so.

If one observes the behavior of those members of our society who are more poorly developed mentally or physically, one will notice that they exaggerate their participation in activities which for them symbolize adulthood—being grown-up. They may end up as alcoholics, chain-smokers, nymphomaniacs, or Don Juans. Exaggeration in the imitation of grown-up activities is a sign of a feeling of incompleteness. Today millions find pleasure in smok-

"These attitudes opened the gates to rape, prostitution, sexual violence, and perversion of sex, particularly in the human male."

ing or drinking. It all started when, as a child or an adolescent, they copied what they considered the proper activity of an "adult." Any time a smoker or a drinker doubts his completeness he needs encouragement. This he finds in successfully performing a "grown-up" activity, such as lighting a cigarette. Any time frigid men or women doubt their maturity they will quickly indulge in sexual activity—a performance considered "grown-up" —in search of self-reassurance.

In humans, sex became a yardstick of achievement, an instrument of completeness—a means of satisfaction. These attitudes opened the gates to rape, prostitution, sexual violence, and perversion of sex, particularly in the human male. In the animal world there is no such thing as rape, prostitution, or perversion.

Mankind's beginnings were based on the immature instinct for reproduction among some apes. As this deficiency, owing to the early mortality of our human ancestors (they lived for about twenty to twenty-five years), had no time to improve, it slowly became part of their nature.

The offspring of these new couples, if similar to the parents, would stay with them on the fringes of the main group.

Darwin realized that humans evolved from inferior apes, but he did not dare to emphasize the fact. It was already considered a crime in his time to have revealed that man and ape had common ancestors. "Hence it might have been an immense advantage to man to have sprung from comparatively weak creatures," he wrote in *The Descent of Man*. "We have seen," he wrote in the same book, "in the last two chapters that man bears in his bodily structure clear traces of his descent from some lower form."

Today, when man is so proud of his achievements, he still produces non-self-sufficient, incomplete infants, who, not inheriting any natural pattern of behavior, have to learn how to live. Man had to invent cultural inheritance, which is an imitation of the past. Cultural inheritance is not a natural inheritance; it is an "ought to be" behavior; it has to be forced on human infants.

The ancient Egyptian Ani advised his son to marry and beget a son whom he must "teach to be a man." Since the beginning of his existence in the woodlands, man has had to learn how to be a man. The Egyptian deity's advice was as valid in the woodlands as it is today in British schools or in Sicilian villages.

The human reproducton continued, not as a result of instinct but by an imitation of sexual intercourse and the pleasure experienced in successful imitation. When one sees a little girl playing with dolls it is a result of her developed instinct of imitation, not her instinct for reproduction.

With pregnancy our human female ancestors acquired the instinct of preservation of the species, particularly in caring for their offspring.

With the birth of the offspring of the two original underdeveloped apes, the first nucleus of mankind was formed. The female soon realized that the only way to keep the male with her and the group was sexual pleasure. The new group introduced a new way of life to the world of mammals, a life of sexual promiscuity based on consensus which, as any consensus, was based on seduction. In the case of our ancestors, it was the seduction of the male by the female.

Man, an animal with a feeling of insufficiency, found self-importance in sexual intercourse, a feeling of achievement. This is why sex was and still is performed throughout the year, day and night.

The first human society based on sexual pleasure was dominated by woman. In promiscuity, paternity is unknown. The human female, thrown into this group of abulic omega apes, recognized that she had to seduce them and keep them under the spell of seduction. The human female, compared to her cousin the ape who attracts males by the scent of her oestrus, developed her own intuition, the ability to smell out the easiest prey among men. Here an important factor must be emphasized. The human female, in order to seduce the male, followed the elementary law of movement in nature, the law of least resistance. The female was attracted to the male who proved the easiest to seduce. This is why the theory of natural and sexual selection have never worked with the human species.

Spurred on by numbers, our ancestors, still living alongside their cousins the apes, performed the first and most important act of mankind. They rebelled. They rebelled against following the main group which up to that time had always been natural. They separated from the main group, from authority, from natural order (an order based on the dominance of the fittest), and started an autonomous life, a life of sexual pleasure in sexual permissiveness.

This first step of mankind, this rebellion against natural order based on the authority of the fittest, has left a big scar on the old brain of humanity. This scar shaped the human mind when it became active in Homo sapiens.

Any hierarchy, whether religious, social, economic or political, became the reason for rebellion, the *movens* of revolution for male humanity, as soon as the power of the mind was discovered. Individuals, and gangs of individuals, lived, and still live in permanent fear of being taken over by some superior individual or a superior gang. Humans achieved a paradox typical of their species. They were able to accept misery with joy as long as everyone was sharing it equally. The old Italian proverb *Mal comune, mezzo gaudio* (An evil in common is halfway to enjoyment) has proved valid throughout history. This paradox of the human mind, this fear of being overtaken by someone fitter, can be seen in the success of the systems that promise equality, even if equality is misery.

If any animal could ever achieve abstract thought, the idea of rebellion would never enter its mind. For an animal, rebellion is abnormal and dangerous. The animal world must have viewed the first rebellion of the human species, and any subsequent rebellion, as humans view rebellious cancerous cells reproducing independently, defying any order or limit on their growth, and breaking the harmony and eventually the existence of the organism in which they live—their own habitat.

Rebellion and the search for autonomy will always remain the essence of human nature, the nature of the inferior being. Rebellion is in conflict with rational laws. Humans, when they discovered the mind, even glorified rebellions and revolutions. Men dedicated one of the most important myths to their greatest rebel, Prometheus.

Human beings were the victims of natural selection, and essentially they will always hate inequality. Most human rebellions were successful because they were fought in the name of equality. Equality is irrational, and irrationality is stronger than rationality because it is accompanied by aggression.

An inferior being can only succeed by destroying order. The history of mankind is only a history of social, political, economic, and religious rebellions, rebellions of the inferior—inferior in age, wealth, strength, or intelligence; rebellions in the name of equality. Humans, after all, are only happy when promiscuous and permissive because this gives them the impression of freedom, of access to all ranks, so canceling all ranks. The first human community was a community of "hippie apes" who eschewed law and order and formed their own independent commune.

Humans owe their survival as a species to the pleasures of mating. The purpose of mating in the animal world, dictated by an instinct, is to promulgate the species. The purpose of mating in humans is pleasure, through which, by accident, the human species has continued. The natural instinct for reproduction has its counterpart. It diminishes or ceases whenever the number of individuals increases to the point of jeopardizing the survival of the species. The reproduction of humans, based on sexual pleasure, and on mental satisfaction after the mind was discovered, has no natural brakes. This must be emphasized in order to explain the next major happening in the history of mankind.

In the Oligocene epoch, between 25–36 million years ago, there is already a clear distinction between apes and humans living side by side in the woodlands of Africa. The ancestors of gorillas and chimpanzees, respecting the natural law of selective reproduction, advanced in their evolution. Our human ancestors, particularly human males, living their lives of pleasure in an environment ideal from the point of view of climate, security and food, and devoid of competition for sex, lagged behind the apes. In this earthly paradise, our human ancestors played with life. Toleration by apes of humans was guaranteed through the amount of food and space available in the Oligocene period, which also was the most ideal epoch for primates in its climate.

Life in the Oligocene paradise left a deep mark on the old brain of our human ancestors, a mark which has been bequeathed to all our descendents and will continue to be bequeathed over future millennia, a mark which will shape, feed, and influence the thoughts of the human mind: Paradise.

In this life of paradise, the human male lost the remainder of his instinct of aggression—his canine teeth. In promiscuity, where there is no sexual selection or discrimination, aggression and authority are replaced by seduction and consensus. Humans, these unaggressive animals, soon began to fear even the sight of a display of strength or signs of aggression from their cousins the apes.

In the Oligocene epoch, human ancestors and ape ancestors lived together in peaceful co-existence. The apes evolved in a natural way, conducive to natural selection; humans evolved in a promiscuous way guided by sexual pleasure. Promiscuous reproduction created variety, and in this variety of human types we must look for an important factor in the survival of humans as a species, particularly when they started life in the savannah. In the animal world the fittest reproduce, in this way helping the species to survive. The animal's way of survival is better for a stable environment and for animals who are specialized. The human's way was better for unspecialized animals and for the unpredictable and changing environment which humans faced in the savannah.

In the Miocene epoch, 13–26 million years ago, the second major event occurred in the evolution of mankind; a change of climate took place. The deterioration of the climate transformed a great part of the woodlands into a desert. This new environment brought major changes to the existence of the primates. Previously the vastness of the woodlands and the abundance of food enabled the primates to tolerate each other. There was no territorial feeling. When the space for living was reduced, non-toleration by apes of humans began. Reduction in food and space created an awareness of territory, and this awareness bred aggression.

Here I repeat that the instinct for reproduction in animals brings with it its own automatic brakes, whenever the environment cannot support the increase in population. In humans then, as today, since reproduction was not controlled by instinct but by pleasure, there were no brakes. Instead, for some abnormal or typically human reason, in any situation of anxiety or danger, humans copulate more avidly—and so increase their population.

Soon the war between apes and humans became open and total. Humans, in their ever increasing numbers, were creating a serious threat to the survival of the apes. The apes, however, were better equipped for the battle. They had "abided" by natural selection, by which the fittest survive for reproduction, and had developed their main weapons, canine teeth. Humans no longer possessed these aggressive tools. Apes became territorial animals and started to chase humans, first to the edge of the woodlands, then out to the open savannah. Humans had never developed their sense of territory; they had no natural weapons—and therefore no aggressive instinct to defend it. In promiscuity there is no feeling of property or territory. Humans, as we shall see later, started to develop a feeling of territory with the arrival of Homo sapiens—with the first man-made weapons. We shall also see later that human aggression developed *pari passu*, with the development of the human mind.

About 16 million years ago our ancestors were evicted from their woodland paradise into the hell of the African savannah. This traumatic experience, this ejection from paradise, has remained as a scar in mankind's brain for eternity.

Most anthropologists assert that human stock, the brightest of existing animals, came one day out of its natural, ideal environment, with food in abundance and no danger, and chose to start a new life in the hell of the savannah, with limited food, no safe shelter, and a savannah filled with dangerous predators and particularly deadly serpents, which humans and apes feared—and still fear hysterically. This theory is not acceptable by any natural logic. No animal will voluntarily leave a good environment for a bad one. This cannot be explained by the logic of our ancestors—a logic dictated by sexual pleasure, a pleasure more safely performed in the woodlands than in the perilous savannah. These explanations follow modern human logic, which is based on conceit. Humans, considering themselves the most advanced species in nature, had to proclaim that this important step was the most progressive step of their ancestors, determined by free will (which is mankind's great illusion).

As we shall see, the human brain started to expand fast only about a million years ago, and only became capable of abstract thought and conceit about 30,000 years ago. Our ancestors,

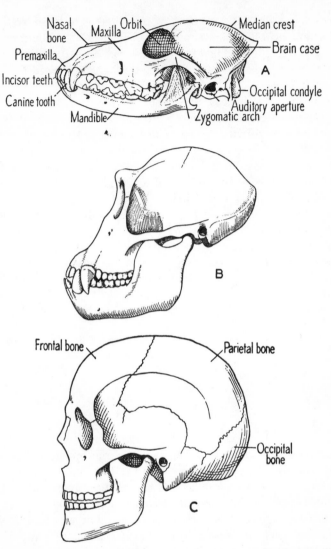

The skull of a dog, a chimpanzee and Man, showing the contrast in the relative proportions of different parts. "The apes . . . 'abided' by natural selection . . . and had developed their main weapons, canine teeth. Humans no longer possessed these aggressive tools."

therefore, could not have been so conceited as to be so irrational.

I think that the most compelling evidence that humans were evicted from the woodlands into the savannah is the fact that the human mind, when it started to function, created the idea of paradise. The mind's ability to create was influenced by the scars left on the brain by past experiences of the species. If any other animal ever became capable of creating abstract ideas, it would never imagine paradise. It would never be able to summon up the myth of a Golden Age. Paradise arises from an experience of humiliation which animals never face. No animal has ever been thrown out of its environment and survived.

Mankind is the product neither of fallen angels nor elevated apes. Mankind consists of fallen apes. The Bible is more accurate than science in its explanation of the origin of human life. Our human ancestors, our Adams and Eves, were evicted from Paradise. The only difference is that historically they were not evicted by Almighty God, but by fitter apes.

Life in the Savannah

Most historians ignore the gap between the appearance of our human ancestors in the savannah to the last million years there, evading the problems of the millions of years intervening. Desmond Morris in *The Naked Ape*, after indulging himself for about one page on this period, moves at once to the following statement: "This brings us to the last million or so years of the naked ape's ancestral history, and to a series of shattering and increasingly dramatic developments" . . . "the ancestral ground apes already had large and higher quality brains. They had good eyes and efficient grasping hands. They inevitably, as primates, had some degree of social organisation. With strong pressure on them to increase their prey-killing prowess, vital changes began to take place. They became more upright—fast, better runners. Their hands became freed from locomotion duties—strong, efficient weapon-holders. Their brain became more complex—brighter, quicker decision-makers. These things did not follow one another in a major set sequence; they blossomed together, minute advances being made first in one quality and then in another, each urging the other one. A hunting ape, a killer ape was in the making."

To me, it seems, mankind in the savannah was pathetic. These years of pathetic misery registered in mankind's brain and helped humans when they were able to think in abstract terms to create the idea of humaneness, another peculiarity of mankind.

We know that Australopithecus, who lived approximately a million and a half years ago, was about four feet tall with a brain capacity between 435–600 cubic centimeters, much the same as today's gorilla. Australopithecus' forebears, when they first came to the savannah about 16 million years ago, could not have been more than two feet six inches tall, with a brain a third of the size of today's gorilla. This frightened and feeble underdeveloped creature, by nature defenseless, and with no special talent or aptitude for life in his new environment, makes a laughingstock of the theories of most anthropologists.

But this human frailty and lack of specialization, in fact, became the main prop for survival in the savannah. If humans had been stronger and more specialized, like any other specialized animal in a new environment, they would have exhausted the potentialities of their specialization to an extreme degree, and become extinct as a species. Specialization has a quality of perseverance, which in any unnatural environment is fatal. As Russell stresses, an animal insists on following his instinct, either to his goal, or to his death.

By the close of the Miocene era, the basic human stock was living in the savannah, about to confront the Pliocene epoch, which lasted 13–1 million years ago. This was the most testing time in the history of mankind—an era of climatic deterioration and droughts which transformed Africa into a graveyard for many species. This climatically aggressive situation left a deep scar on the human old brain, a scar which influenced the mind in its creation of the first idea of hell. It says, in the Sumerian epic

Inanna's Journey to Hell: "Here is no water but only rock, rock and no water and the sandy road" . . . In *The Epic of Gilgamesh* the writer states that "Hell is frightening because of its sandy dust" and because it is "the dead land" . . . It is "the river which has no water." In *Inanna's Journey to Hell,* when the goddess Inanna is revived from the dead and is ready to return to the land of the living, one of the judges of the nether world says: "Who has ever returned out of Hell unharmed?"

The variety of human types created by promiscuity was an advantage for the survival of the human species. Variety, or diversity in human individuals, helped, helps and will help humanity as a species to survive, as long as the fact is faced that humans lack an innate pattern of behavior and always face the threat of a change in environment. Some human individuals or groups, however abnormal they may appear to human assumptions of aesthetic, racial, psychological, or biological points of view, should never be suppressed by the majority of "normals." The suppression of the "inferior" by the "superior" threatens the continuation of the human species. With the possibility of continual change in the natural and cultural environment of mankind, anyone could (with reservations) be the "fittest." Any a priori, and even a posteriori meaning given to the idea of the fittest is ill advised, owing to the lack of specialization in the human species, and owing to the unpredictability of cultural and natural events.

Humans entered their new environment with no natural ability for surviving and with their instincts weakened by their hedonistic life. This lack of survivability urged them toward what became another peculiarity: improvisation. A specialized animal in a new environment is guided by his specialization; humans were guided by external circumstances.

What was the human group organization in the savannah?

With insecurity and anxiety about living, all manners of sensual pleasures developed. When men discovered the brain they added pleasures of the mind to sexual and sensual pleasures. Men have always been unscrupulous pursuers of pleasure and will remain so until one man, as a result of personal pleasure, triggers off a universal weapon that wipes out the entire species. Man is the only animal who kills for pleasure.

In the savannah, man's sex urge increased; even modern man's sex urge increases when anxious or panic-struck. During the Second World War those closest to the front line were obsessed by sex. Christian Europe was densely populated in the tenth century because the people feared the end of the world at the close of the first millennium.

In the savannah a phenomenon of great importance in the evolution of mankind occurred. The human male passed through a retrograde metamorphosis. He reverted to infancy. Even modern male, with all his intricately developed mental capacities, will, after any failure, revert to infancy. It is as if he wanted to become a child again in order to grow up and prepare himself all the better for a new life.

Our male ancestors started life in the savannah by regressing to neoteny, paedomorphosis, or to the Peter Pan evolutionary phase. In neoteny, the human male remained childlike in character all his life.

It was not a big backward step for man. He emerged from the woodlands, not only unspecialized but biologically retarded, and with weakened instincts, all attributable to his previously idyllic existence.

Many scientists agree that in the early stages there was an infantile phase in the savannah. Their belief is that it was mankind, both men and women, who went through this phase. It is my contention that if this were the case, we would not exist as a species today. It would have contradicted the elementary law of nature if a mother returned to infancy. A woman matures with pregnancy and acquires a feeling of responsibility toward the species. So in nature, the initiative and responsibility of the species belongs to the female.

The first historical evidence of a human mother suckling her infant comes from ancient Egypt, where, it is recorded, a child was breast-fed until it was three years old. In the savannah, many millions of years earlier, the child must have been breast-fed for much longer, and therefore for almost the greater part of man's life—man's life span then being much shorter.

Many scientists write in one paragraph that mankind faced a phase of infancy, often dedicating the next paragraph to the domineering and glorious male hunter, the generous and brave

"Infancy assumes play."

provider of food for his family. Infancy means dependence; infancy needs a mother, a mother's guidance. The instinct system in infancy is confused and unreliable, even in animals with a strong system of built-in reactions. The infant has to learn; the human infant even more so owing to his lack of specialization. The mother teaches him. Humans achieved a cultural instead of genetic transmission of patterns of behavior.

With the human males as infants, mankind in the savannah continued to be dominated by women.

What does reverting to infancy mean in practical terms? Infancy assumes play. The human species owes its survival to play. Being an activity which explores the environment and is guided by curiosity (fed by what Schiller called "exuberant energy" typical in all infants, and in particular human infants), play has brought mankind to its most typical discovery: opportunism.

This permanent desire for new experiences, paramount in infancy through a greater sense of inquiry, became part of the nature of human males. It will always be nourished—for men feel that the new environment is not their natural one, but merely temporary, through which, by exploration, they will sooner or later find their lost paradise.

Curiosity, it seems, is a dispersion of nervous energy through the open senses. Man has more curiosity than other animals, not because he has more nervous energy, but because he has more open senses. Through these permanently open senses his nervous energy is in continuous contact with the external world. This nervous energy is never concentrated in one sense because the other senses remain open. Man might be compared with a sea monster with several extended feelers, feelers of different shapes, moving in all directions (movements inherited from life in the trees) to explore.

Man will always feel like a "tourist" in the new environment, a tourist in search of a temporary settlement. He will never involve himself wholeheartedly into any activity or specialization, as the feeling of *provisoire* dictates the motto of his life, "be prepared" —always ready for a new environment, another situation, another expulsion. Besides, for man, a biologically incomplete being, anything in nature can be put to some use. Even today, man, after a failure, never throws away a new chance.

That man considered existence in the savannah temporary is evident in that as soon as he discovered the creativity of his mind, he invented Paradises, Kingdoms of Heaven, Kingdoms of Gods and Utopias.

A specialized animal has at any one time only one sensor shaped, for the dispersion of its nervous energy. This nervous energy ignores whatever does not accommodate the expectations of its open sensor. Young animals, because of their underdeveloped stage, are more curious than their parents.

Less specialized animals are more vulnerable, and therefore more curious. Highly specialized animals are rarely curious. Some people believe that curiosity is the result of intelligence. Both are the result of vulnerability and insecurity.

Exploratory play, an elastic, incomplete, and experimental activity, is what men will lean on to discover the best adaptation to their new environment. Play is, after all, the only activity which suits the nature of an incomplete animal such as man—an animal suffering from insufficiency. Play, which includes imitation, became man's only specialization, because it was the easiest way of adjusting to the variety of life in the new environment.

Huizinga considered that play was an irrational activity. We may consider it an irrational activity, but only because in our self-infatuation we consider ourselves purposeful, superior beings, beings with a self-acquired specialization, and with important roles in life. But despite our self-infatuation we are still simple opportunists, and play is the only rational activity for an opportunist; it is in keeping with his nature. The life of an opportunist is learning, permanent learning which can only be achieved through play. Learning, improvisation, and elasticity; these pre-eminent attributes of an opportunist are only possible through play. What is more, through play and exploration an opportunist achieves the essential and permanent aim of an unspecialized animal: to widen his living space. Here can be seen the rationality of play. Its purpose is to widen the possibilities for the life and survival of an opportunist. Any serious or purposeful activity in the new environment would have risked a clash, in which the loser would have been man.

In the savannah man felt imprisoned, as any animal in a new environment. With imprisonment even mature and specialized animals resort to play; probably because it is the only activity left to them in their desperate search for a means of survival.

This life of opportunism, discovered through play, had an important effect in perpetuating man's infancy for several million years. A life of exploratory play is filled with danger and accidents. Nature is not playful. Whenever man in play met the determination of a mature situation, or the result of a specialization, he would flee and run to his mother for protection, for encouragement, and for a new dose of infancy. Infants know only one reality: that of play; any other reality frightens them. The short life of humans in those days is another factor which perpetuated infancy in human males.

Human female found herself in the savannah with her maternal instinct of care for the young greatly increased owing to the male reversion to infancy. Even today man is by nature a dependent animal: in infancy he is guided by his mother; in adolescence by supernatural infatuation, by abstract ideas, or by beliefs. We will see later that man has never fully matured.

In the savannah, our mothers' ancestors soon developed, probably through their maternal instinct, the gift which has always remained with them: their easy adaptability to new circumstances. Woman was helped in her easy adaptability by her enhanced instinct for imitation.

From the start of their life in the savannah, man and woman behaved differently toward the environment. Man wanted to explore, and woman exploited his explorations. Man discovered how best to exploit circumstances; woman adapted herself to them.

Play taught mankind another lesson: "Nothing in excess." Millions of years later this became the motto at Delphi. Play helped humans in another way too. When they came out of the woodlands they were already individually more differentiated than any other species, through their sexual promiscuity. In the new environment play helped these individuals to develop their differences, the differences which contributed to the survival of mankind as a species. Faced with any new circumstance, there would always be at least one individual who would be able to face it somehow.

Play soon became a pleasure in itself. It suited human nature. It was the incomplete activity of an incomplete being. An incomplete activity leaves an unsatiated curiosity behind it. When animals play it is merely an exercise for their instincts and a training for their specialization. Play ceases with the start of their biological maturity. The animal and human infant share hiding and fleeing in common. These teach the most valuable behavior in nature. Escaping or hiding from danger is a natural and wise precaution. Only man (paradoxically only when man discovered his brain, or more precisely when he discovered his mind) has ever started to provoke danger. Courage has killed more men than anything else. Man considers courage a virtue. Animals consider it against nature, and therefore most unwise.

Man remained in this phase of childhood throughout the Pliocene epoch, which extended for nearly 12 million years. The reason for this protracted childhood was the continuing frustration of an opportunist's life in deteriorating climatic conditions.

The behavior of human beings today in certain revolutions and catastrophes is comparable to the behavior of our human ancestors in the savannah. A rejected or displaced person is closer to our human ancestors than a human fossil or an aborigine could ever be. One could compare our ancestors, evicted from the woodlands, with displaced persons after the Second World War, when the women immediately adapted themselves to their new life and environment, while the men very often reverted to infancy. When these rejected men were interviewed by immigration officers in America, they were like lost children, answering the question "What will you do in America?" with "Anything."

The economic miracle in Italy after the Second World War can be explained by the metamorphosis of the Italian men. After defeat and the fall of Fascism (and therefore the deflation of their self-infatuation), they reverted to infancy. They acquired a childlike enthusiasm and an eagerness to learn. Many authors have tried to explain the miraculous recovery of the Germans and the Japanese after defeat. Recognition of the failure of their adolescent self-infatuation brought them back to infancy and its optimism. In the case of the Germans we must also remember the infantile enthusiasm of the refugees from the East. And would England have become such a prosperous and industrialized country without the infantile enthusiasm such as that of the Hu-

guenot immigrants? The economic productivity of th
worker and his achievements at the end of the nineteе
beginning of the twentieth century were largely due
thusiasm of immigrants who had been rejected from all ᴏ
world for political, economic, or religious reasons. What is more,
these American immigrants, just like our ancestors in the savannah, thought that their new life was only temporary. This gave
America the rush and hurry which accelerated its rhythm of life.

After the 1917 Russian revolution, universities all over the
world became inundated by Russian refugees. They were more
youthful and enthusiastic than their young colleagues.

How many men today, afraid or disillusioned by the modern
world of corruption, hypocrisy, and chicanery, prefer to revert
to infancy and play with their own special noisy toys: sports
cars, guns, and bombs, liable to cause all manner of social and
economic disturbances or revolutions. Disturbances or revolutions have one thing in common with play: they have no purpose. *They* are the purpose. Nietzsche said that in every adult
man "is hiding a child who wants to play."

It is very probable that the reason why human beings have a
longer childhood than any other species of animal is due to man's
reversion to infancy during the millions of years in the savannah.
In the rest of the mammalian world infancy and prepuberty, the
period between birth and sexual maturity, is, on average, a tenth
to a twelfth part of the animal's whole life. For humans, until
only a few centuries ago, it was nearly half their whole life. This
long infancy, however, was vital to the life of an opportunist. An
opportunist, without any innate pattern of behavior to help him,
has to learn how to live. Perhaps this explains why an infant human's brain is only 23 per cent of its adult size, compared with 40
per cent in an infant orang-utan, 45 per cent in an infant chimpanzee and 59 per cent in an infant gorilla. One year after birth, a
chimpanzee's brain is fully grown. Some monkeys complete their
brain growth within six months of birth. On average, humans
take twenty-three years fully to develop theirs.

In their incompleteness, our ancestors found an ally to aid
them in their survival in the savannah. Unconsciously, humans
played the great game of nature; the display of strength. In this
game, the survival of the least fit is guaranteed by his withdrawal

at the first sign of a greater display of strength. Unexpectedly meeting dangerous predators, and being unable to escape, the humans would suddenly collapse, their bodies giving all signs of death. This apparent death was caused then, as it is caused today, by sudden terror. The muscles in the walls of the periferic blood vessels contract, blocking the flow of blood to the periferic organs of the human body, thus directing it to the vital central organs. As the arteria vertebralis and the arteria carotis and their branches, which supply blood to the brain are the periferic blood vessels, they contract, thereby stopping the blood coming to the brain, causing the syncope.

Life in the savannah meant organization and a division of labor. The female-dominated human group would find a protected spot under some isolated trees where the home would be formed and life would be organized. Mothers with offspring would hang from the branches, while the males went off in search of food. Man started life in the savannah by food gathering, bringing it back to his group in exchange for protection and sexual pleasure. Over the past millions of years, man has not changed. If man had not been in infancy, therefore dependent on women, and if his instinct for survival had been stronger than his need for biological comforts, he would never have returned with the food. With other primates, the group follows the males.

Even today, after millions of years of cultural, moral, and religious influence, man only shares what is his in return for comfort and security. From the earliest legal codes to the present there is a repetition of judicial norms which impose duties on man as far as the family's maintenance is concerned.

Man's selfishness increased during his phase of infancy. The females, aware of this characteristic, introduced a positive rule in their relationship: the rule of *Do ut des*. Man needed protection, comfort, and sexual pleasure; woman provided these in return for the food brought to her and the group. The more comfort or sexual pleasure he demanded, the harder he had to work for it.

A man today, away from home and away from the cultural, moral, or legal obligations imposed on him by his group, might behave in the same way as did his ancestors in the savannah. But instead of bringing food to earn his comforts and pleasure, he

MAN: THE FALLEN APE

would take a woman out for dinner, hoping for the best afterward. He might even come to a financial arrangement from the start. Prostitution is another peculiarity of the human species.

Sharing food is indeed not in man's nature, and it is interesting to notice that men in the hippie communes of today are more generous with their priceless marijuana than with food.

The human group was dominated by a hierarchical order of females established by age. The eldest women were in charge.

In the savannah the older women used their memory, important factors in the life of a species that had to learn how to live. Before man became aware of his brain, he was still in the infancy phase, and infants, even when they develop a memory, seldom rely on it. In infants curiosity is stronger than memory. In order to rely on the memory, humans must acquire self-confidence. The hierarchical position produced this self-confidence.

Another proof that women must have been in charge of the human groups up until the adolescent revolution, which started about 25,000 years ago, is the human male's lack of efficient canine teeth. He must have lost them 20 million years ago during his *dolce vita* in the woodlands. Canine teeth in the animal world serve either for duels in the intra-specific selection with other males, or for fighting the enemies of the species for the protection of the young. In the mammalian world one of the supreme aims of the male, and one of the reasons for his existence after insemination of the female, is the protection of the new generation. The fact that man lost his canine teeth so many millions of years ago can have only one meaning, which is, that he did not fight for sexual predominance and that he did not protect the young of the species. After all, one could not ask men in the savannah to defend their infants when they themselves were in an infantile phase.

Humans, the males through exploration, the females through imitating men, became omnivores. Man, like any child who finds something new—eggs, small birds and young animals, insects, roots, plants, berries, meat from carcasses left by other animals— puts them straight into his mouth. By this method of trial and error, mankind discovered the human diet. Judging by the quantity of animal bones and skulls found near human fossils, marrow and brains were clearly part of the human diet. These were the only parts of an animal that predators would not eat.

Most scientists claim that men, as soon as they escaped to the savannah, started hunting, providing food for their families like medieval knights. In our conceit we have produced this romantic fallacy. Later I shall show how man is the only animal capable of self-deception.

One can make nonsense of this question of hunting by asking one simple question: How and with what weapons could man have hunted? As the spear was not invented until 30,000 years ago and the bow and arrow not until 12–15,000 years ago, I fail to see how this was possible. Man started his life in the savannah with neither natural nor artificial weapons. Hunting is an activity either dictated by instinct or by abstract thought, and man, prior to Homo sapiens, had neither. In his sheltered life of the woodland, he had lost his keen sense of smell, inherited from lower mammals. In the trees he had developed his sight; but in the savannah he needed to be more careful not to be seen, than to be able to see.

The human males food-gathered in packs. They started this by imitating other animals, particularly hyenas. They searched for carcasses killed by some lone predator, whom they would frighten from his feast by their vast numbers—or they would seek out a wounded animal.

Safety in numbers is yet another scar on our old brain which has fed and programed the human new brain, influencing man's creative thoughts. Overpopulation is probably also due to safety in numbers.

In the woodlands, fruit and leaves, plus the morning dew, was sufficient to quench human thirst. In the savannah humans became dependent on a source of drinking water, and could never stray far from lakes or rivers. Millions of years later, with the agricultural revolution of approximately the eighth millennium B.C., the first fixed settlements were founded near sources of drinking water.

Humans were weak, miserable, and clumsy creatures in the savannah of Africa, but a positive element was concealed in their weakness and clumsiness. Perhaps, when the brain started to create proverbs, this misery inspired the saying: "Good can come out of bad," a proverb repeated by mankind throughout history. Suddenly this unspecialized, unpredictable animal, this clumsy, unco-ordinated, and inarticulate being in his unnatural environment, this discord in the natural harmony, became a frightening creature to other animals. Man became something to avoid, an attitude that animals adopt even today.

What is paradoxical is that these abnormal creatures, through their exploration of nature, learned a lesson: "Beware of freaks of nature." Disharmony in nature causes abnormal reactions. Harmony is harmless. "Beware of freaks of nature" was transformed by the ancient Romans into a moral rule, with their popular saying: *Cave a signatis.*

In Greek mythology Perseus kills Medusa. He is frightened by her ugliness.

"Life in the savannah initiated another metamorphosis—a meta-morphosis which presented humans with another peculiarity: nakedness."

Human Nakedness

Life in the savannah initiated another metamorphosis—a metamorphosis which presented humans with another peculiarity: nakedness. Why and how humans lost their hair has always been an enigma. In *The Naked Ape* Desmond Morris claims that humans lost their hair to avoid overheating while hunting. Even accepting the theory that men in the savannah hunted, this would still not explain why the other hunting animals in the savannah did not become likewise naked.

Some writers claim that our hair fell out for aesthetic reasons, making us more attractive to each other. Clearly these authors had in mind beautiful models emerging from bubble baths in Passy or Mayfair, not fat, coarse women covered with sores, boils, and bleeding wounds caused by insect bites or skin diseases.

Many people believe that our ancestors spent a long period as aquatic animals when they left the woodlands, claiming that in the water they would have been better protected from predators. Perhaps they have forgotten that the waters were also filled with dangerous predators. Besides, truly aquatic animals, such as seals and beavers, do not lose their hair. By the same logic one might postulate that humans spent a long period living underground, because worms are hairless.

If the theory that humans spent a period of their evolution in water was true, then the human mind, when it started to create myths, would surely have never imagined the myth of floods. From the first flood described in a Sumerian myth, to that in the Bible, floods appeared as punishments. The Babylonian God Marduk was considered merciful but one "whose rage is a devastating flood."

Scientists claim that human hair fell out because of mankind's sudden eviction from the cool and shady woodlands into the hot, arid plains of the savannah. But this would still not explain why baboons, for instance, have remained hairy. For they too were in the savannah and still are.

Before moving to my own explanation it must be said that human nakedness is neither a positive acquisition nor an improvement. On the contrary. "The loss of hair is an inconvenience, and probably an injury to man, even in a hot climate, for he is thus exposed to the scorching of the sun, and to sudden chill, especially during wet weather," wrote Darwin in *The Descent of Man*. "No-one supposes," he adds, "that the nakedness of the skin is any direct advantage to man."

Human nakedness is a positive abnormality and therefore must have been brought about by abnormal circumstances.

When humans found themselves cast out into the savannah, they soon discovered that the biological adaptation they had brought from the woodlands was not good enough in the new environment. In the woodlands, hunger, the result of the expenditure of energy, was a warning that glucose in the blood had decreased to the point where food was needed. This decrease in glucose triggered off a hormonal mechanism which mobilized the remaining glucose and created energy to search for food. This slow mechanism functioned perfectly in the woodlands where the remaining glucose was enough to help humans find food, since food was abundant and close by.

In the savannah where food was scarce, our ancestors soon realized that their hormonal mechanism was so slow that what glucose they could contain was often insufficient for the energy needed to find food. Because their warning mechanism was inadequate, many of our ancestors perished, and many nearly perished. The experience of being almost too late to obtain food produced a scar on the human old brain, the scar of terror. Around this scar was laid down the first stratum, the foundation of the new human brain, which developed in the savannah. With this stratum we have the beginning of a faster mechanism, the first independent activity of the brain. Humans no longer waited for the decrease in glucose content to start their search for food. Terrified, they conducted a continuous search and as a result began to overeat, and so created reserves. This may be why humans became omnivorous.

The human brain, which developed in the savannah, was influenced by terror. The stratum formed around the scar of terror became a focus of anxiety, permanently reminding the human species of its vulnerability in its unnatural environment. Humans today are able to enter a state of terror and anxiety merely by imagining it. That the development of the human brain was influenced by terror and anxiety can also be deduced by the fact that most mental illnesses are nothing but exaggerated fear and anxiety.

With the anxiety created in the savannah, the human species began to overeat. This overeating soon became a pleasure for the species, because while it was stuffing itself, its anxiety diminished. This pleasure, started 15 million years ago, remains today. We can see it, for example, in the indigenous people of America and Australia who put on weight as soon as they become "integrated" into the new environment imposed by the white man. The human is the only species of animal who will kill itself by overeating and overdrinking. Mankind, with all its illusions of advancement, has never been able to eliminate anxiety. The continuous and increasing demand for tranquilizers and sleeping pills underline this fact.

Overeating, based on anxiety, produced subcutaneous fat—the reserve for uncertainty.

There are two natural protections which keep body temperature at a constant level: fur and fat. In my view, the accumulation of subcutaneous fat in our human ancestors slowly eliminated the external fur. Fat glands were situated between the fur roots and the smooth muscle. In a state of anxiety, contractions of those muscles, pressing the fat glands, pushed the fur out. (Pubic hair roots are not surrounded by fat but by sweat glands.) What is more, during moments of increased fear, blood leaves the skin and the hair roots and accumulates in central or vital organs.

Women, more prone to anxiety than men because of their double responsibility toward their infant offspring and their infantile males, became fatter than men. Even today a woman's body has almost twice the fat as a man's. (On average a woman's body contains 28 per cent fat and a man's 15 per cent.) The first known prehistoric statuettes of women are some proof of the obesity of our ancestors.

I would suggest those who depict our ancestors in the savannah as hairy apes are wrong. Today's human male is hairier than he was in the savannah because then he was so much fatter. Besides, the human male was still in infancy then, which would surely have inhibited the growth of a beard. Prehistoric artists show early man as a beardless subject, not even boasting long hair on his head. After the age of forty-five to fifty, modern man (who lives far longer than our ancestors did), starts growing longer eyebrows, and hair appears in his nostrils and earholes.

Frontal Copulation

In the woodlands our ancestors must have copulated from behind like the other primates.

In the savannah, humans developed yet another peculiarity: frontal copulation.

To some scientists, face to face sex was a "personalized intercourse," more dignified for these superior animals, humans. It would have been beneath their dignity to indulge in the vulgar and impersonal copulation from behind—the position adopted by other mammals. There are many other explanations for this peculiarity. Most of them are farcical. At this level one might propose that frontal intercourse, in the dangerous, open savannah, where predators could appear from anywhere, at any moment, gave humans the ability to keep an all-round vigilance!

Surely it is more probable that the reasons for frontal intercourse stem from the new developments brought about in the savannah. Fear or anxiety drives an infant into the arms of its

"*In the Savannah, humans developed yet another peculiarity: frontal copulation.*"

"*Frontal intercourse, in the dangerous, open Savannah . . . gave humans the ability to keep an all-round vigilance.*"

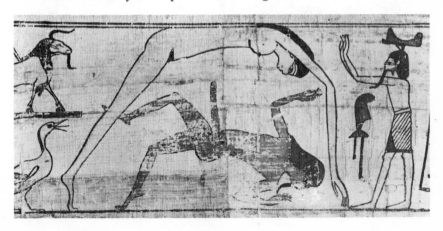

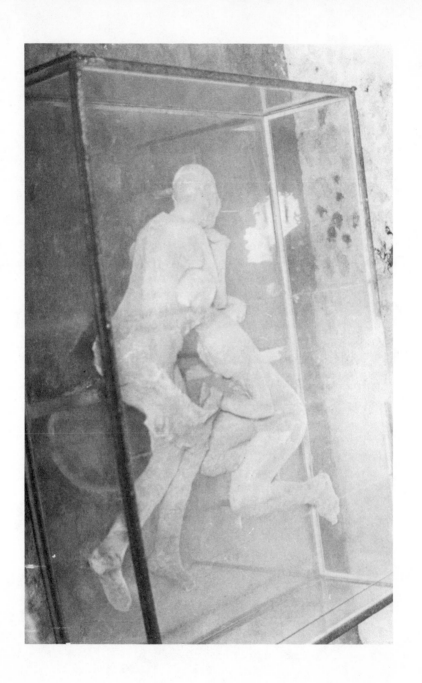

mother or mother-figure. Cuddling was a comfort, as it is today, a comfort increased by the warmth of the fat and by the fat mounds on the female body, built up by the concentration of the extra fat. Round or spherical forms are a sign of harmony and perfection in the eyes of primitive human beings. They inspired security, and induced relaxation. Cuddling reassured these frightened beings. Any creature when frightened reverts to infancy, even if only for a split second, and runs into the first welcoming arms. Human beings will embrace anyone near them, their own sex, even themselves in moments of danger. The greatest monument to the embrace during danger is the skeletons of two people carbonized together by the lava of Vesuvius, in Pompeii.

This comforting and reassuring position of frontal cuddling was the origin, I believe, of frontal copulation. The male, comforted and reassured, got an erection. Sexual intercourse was then almost inevitable. Besides, we must remember that for the human male sexual intercourse is rooted in the need for reassurance of an insecure and incomplete being.

The reason why frontal intercourse remained the preferred position for humans, could be due to the excess of body fat on humans. When the female developed her large buttocks, the male felt that penetration into the vagina was deeper from a frontal position, although even that was not easy. Fat had grown on the stomach and thighs of both sexes. Perhaps this is why man developed the longest penis of all the primates.

The human female found increasing pleasure in frontal intercourse. When cuddling, females find the peace and relaxation essential to their enjoyment of sex. There is an old Slav proverb: "Even if a serpent placed his head against a woman's breast she would stroke it." A female enjoys cuddling. It is part of her maternal instinct. With cuddling she reassures her male or her infant, which to her is like giving a new life.

"Cuddling reassured these frightened beings."

The Human Brain

The period of infancy, or to be more precise of early infancy, in the human male lasted throughout the Pliocene epoch—up to about a million years ago. It lasted so long because of the gradual deterioration in climatic conditions and the feeling of *provisoire*. The past is always a paradise if the present is not.

If the Pliocene age was the epoch of early infancy for the human male, the next epoch, the Pleistocene, lasting from a million years ago until the advent of Homo sapiens (approximately 30,000 years ago) could be considered the period of late infancy or the prepubertal phase.

Toward the beginning of the Pleistocene age, humans were about four feet tall. The capacity of their brain, however, was still only about 600 cubic centimeters, two and a half times smaller than the brain of Homo sapiens, and roughly equal to the brain of today's gorilla.

In the Pleistocene age there were two new phenomena. The first was an extraordinary increase in the size of the human brain; and the second was that humans assumed the erect posture.

In the period from approximately one million years ago to about 200,000 years ago (a very short time in evolutionary terms), the human brain increased its volume by two and a half times.

One of the few writers who have attempted to explain the sudden increase in the size of the brain was Robert Ardrey. In his book *The Social Contract* he wrote: "Seven hundred thousand years ago the earth suffered a violent encounter with a celestial object, perhaps 1,000 ft. in diameter." This "celestial object," which exploded somewhere west of Australia, reversing the

MAN: THE FALLEN APE

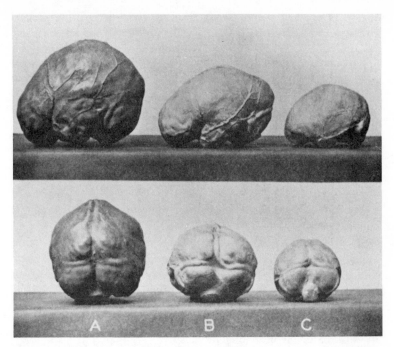

Casts of the inside of the brain-case of Homo sapiens (left), **homo erectus** *(center), and chimpanzee (right). "In the period from approximately one million years ago to about 200,000 years ago (a very short time in evolutionary terms), the human brain increased its volume by two and a half times."*

earth's poles was, in his view, the cause of the extraordinary growth of the human brain. Ardrey, after explaining his "Theory of Man the Cosmic Accident," concluded: "I do so, however, with the strict understanding that I do not believe a word of it." Ardrey is to be admired for his sincerity, but above all for having at least tried to give an answer to the greatest mystery in the history of mankind, an answer carefully avoided by other commentators.

Most scientists claim that the human brain increased as the use of hands increased, which in turn was possible because of human bipedal locomotion. By this theory, humans, in order to increase their brains, needed free hands. To free their hands, they forced themselves to stand upright, to walk on two feet, and to place themselves in a thoroughly unstable and unnatural position. This theory does not explain why it took mankind so many millions of years (15 million approximately) to find out in a flash that they needed the use of their hands. If bipedalism and the use of their hands helped humans to increase their brain, then dinosaurs would still be with us and kangaroos would have a much bigger brain. Extending this theory, our cousins the apes should have bigger brains than they do, judging by their manual dexterity.

But I don't believe it was the use of the hands that increased the brain—it was the reverse.

What then could have been the reason for the increase in the human brain?

The beginning of the Pleistocene age brought an end to the infernal drought in the African savannah, and introduced new climatic conditions, more promising and more encouraging. It started to rain. The abundance of vegetation produced food in plenty. This reawakened enthusiasm and confidence within the human male. The human male entered into that important period in the life of an individual or a species, the prepubertal phase. The human male was ready to grow up, to grow the essential organ of an opportunist, his brain. He was waiting for a sign, an awakening signal, which came with the rains of the Pleistocene age.

This increased enthusiasm, curiosity, and excitement of the awakened opportunist, exercised a new and stronger pressure on his brain. The emotions and frustration of this ambitious but incomplete being created the extra gray matter—the extra brain.

The law of nature is that need creates organs, their evolution depending on the evolution of the need. Any organ responds to pressure and work by strengthening or growing, and vice-versa. These prepubertal men needed bigger brains to cope with their increased needs. More curiosity and enthusiasm, connected with the stage of prepuberty, encountered more emotions and frustration, which made the blood flow toward the only instrument of an unspecialized animal, his brain. The already existing brain was no longer good enough for the fast and appropriate reactions needed in the new circumstances discovered by increased curiosity and enthusiasm. Men felt the need for solutions. They wanted something more than simple play. From exploring they wanted to move on to finding; from the pleasure of searching into the satisfaction of discovery; from movement to settlement; from dependence to independence.

What happened to women?

Any increase in men's brain became something to which women had to adapt, thus increasing, *pari passu*, their own brains. The reason for women's brain developing as fast at this stage was also due to its increased role in guiding their new infants, their men, through the perilous stage of prepuberty.

This leads to the conclusion that the brains of man and woman, having been differently shaped, differ in quality. The argument that man's brain is bigger than woman's (1,380 grams as opposed to 1,260 grams), and the argument that woman's brain is bigger, if taking into consideration the brain-body proportions, than that of man, are pointless, because man and woman have two different brains—not structurally, but functionally.

The kind of thoughts that the brain is able to produce, depends on its shape. The difficulties facing it through which the brain has developed are of first importance in determining the kind or quality of thoughts. Man's brain was programed by terror, anxiety, frustration, and humiliation, and by the life of misery of an opportunist who, in order to survive, had to compete with hyenas and vultures. These factors created a typically male brain which, when it started to think in the abstract sense, produced typically male ideas. If an ape ever reached the stage of discovering an ability for abstract thought, his thinking would be of a different kind, or another quality. No specialized animals, however, will ever discover their brain and start thinking in abstract terms. If animals ever became aware of their brain, their brain would merely become a tool of their nature, of their specialization.

In this situation, we also have the human female. Her brain will always remain part of, or an instrument of, her specialization, of her nature. Only man, an animal without specialization, without an inner nature, with a feeling of insufficiency or incompleteness, could have used his brain to produce a supernature, an abstract world which, by its definition is in contrast with true nature.

A large number of scientists agree, as we have already mentioned, that humanity in the savannah entered a phase of neoteny. They never explain however, when mankind emerged from this stage. From a consideration of neoteny, all scientists move straight to Homo sapiens, who for them represents adult mankind. They evade three important periods in both the life of the human individual and the life of mankind; the periods of prepuberty, puberty, and adolescence.

The prepubertal phase is important because it is when the brain reached 90 per cent of its total volume.

The pubertal phase is important because it is the period of shame, the period of concealing the first signs of puberty. The Latin words *puber* or *pubes* mean to cover or to be clothed. By covering themselves, humans assumed a role, a role determined by the shape or color of the clothes. Shame begins with the discovery of the mind. It lasts until man overcomes his doubts, until, with the appearance of beliefs, he acquires self-confidence. Shame returns whenever self-confidence and beliefs are shaken, whenever man is stripped of them.

The adolescent phase is important because it is when man discovered the power of his mind, the power of self-infatuation, the power of beliefs.

Homo Erectus

Another great mystery in the history of mankind is why and how humans became bipedal creatures, why and how Homo became erectus. Some writers explain this change as the need to free the hands to use tools and weapons. But I believe that man did not begin to use weapons until long after he had been standing upright, and that, for a long time in his new posture, man

MAN: THE FALLEN APE

continued to be only a food-gatherer. Tools, such as they were at the beginning of man's bipedalism, were used with equal dexterity by apes, who did not become bipedal. Thus, handling tools and weapons is not enough of a reason for man to continue walking on two feet and standing upright, tiring things in themselves, at a time when he had no special need to use his hands.

Desmond Morris explains the upright posture by stressing that "with strong pressure on them to increase their prey-killing prowess, they [humans] became more upright, fast, better runners."

But, if man had had "strong pressure" on him to increase his prowess in hunting, why, for all those millions of years, did he not try to improve his running on four legs in order to compete with the speedy four-legged predators? If the pressure had been so strong, he could have done it by imitation instead of choosing the clumsy and low bipedal locomotion. Before athletic games were invented in Greece, and above all in modern sport, man never achieved any speed compared with other predators, particulary those he had to face in the savannah.

Robert Ardrey explains that "we learnt to stand erect in the first place as a necessity for the hunting life."

If one accepted Morris's and Ardrey's explanations of the reasons for the upright posture, the human female would still be on all fours.

Some writers explain that man became upright because from this new posture he could spot his prey more easily. My answer to this is that it is more in keeping with natural logic that a highly vulnerable creature like man, with no offensive or defensive weapons, and lacking the speed of other animals, would have been much more worried about being seen by his predators than spotting his prey.

The instinct of hiding, developing all manner of camouflage, is a part of animal nature. When man started thinking he created man-made camouflage by imitating animals.

Improvisation, which is in the nature of an opportunist, is more difficult in the precarious bipedal position than on all fours.

What happened then? To understand what I am proposing, one must take into consideration the fact that the upright posture coincided with the accelerated increase in the volume, therefore the weight, of the developing human brain. The phases of gradual bipedalism followed the stages of the gradual increase in the size of the brain. And so it would seem that the human erect posture was due to the extra weight in the head. Erect posture was not a choice of man but was forced on him. It was forced on him by the extra weight—approximately 800 grams—of the new brain.

It may seem unbelievable that this small weight could have produced such consequences. It would probably have been irrelevant had it been carried on four legs for a short time; but for a long time, coupled with the exhaustion of living in the savannah, this small weight felt enormous.

My proposition may be understood better from the following examples. An Italian bicycling champion told me that after eight hours of pedaling, hunched over the low handlebars, he felt as if the medal of the Madonna, which hung round his neck on a fine chain, weighed a ton.

Any boxer at the end of the fight will tell you what a relief it is to take off his heavy gloves.

A pregnant woman always stands with her back arched, and wears flat shoes in order to keep the center of gravity in the right place.

Under the pressure of the increased weight of their brain, humans had to either stand upright, balancing the head on the spinal cord, or to develop their shoulder muscles at least two and a half times to stop the head from dropping down. This latter solution would not have been in the nature of opportunists. It would have made them awkward, heavier and slower, which would have been a major handicap in a life of improvisation, a life which needed quick reactions and elastic movements.

Darwin was very close to agreeing with this explanation of the erect posture. "The gradually increasing weight of the brain and skull in man must have influenced the development of the supporting spinal column, more especially whilst he was becoming erect," he wrote in *The Descent of Man*. "In young persons whose heads have become fixed, either sideways or backwards, owing to disease, one of the two eyes has changed its position

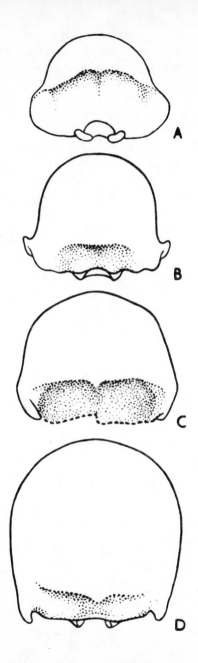

The skulls, seen from behind, of (a) a chimpanzee, (b) one of the Australopithecinae, *(c)* Homo erectus, *and (d)* Homo sapiens. *"Erect posture was . . . forced on [man] by the extra weight— approximately 800 grams—of the new brain."*

and the shape of the skull has been altered apparently by the pressure of the brain, in a new direction," he adds.

Scientists say that when a baby stops crawling and begins trying to walk on two feet, he is urged on by an instinct for bipedalism. Instincts, like gods, are used as easy solutions to cover up ignorance of the real causes.

If bipedalism was an instinct or an innate posture, then the human infant would not take so long to walk on two legs. In the animal world the infant assumes the natural posture of its species a few days after its birth, and in some cases, after only a few hours. If bipedalism were an innate position for man, then humans would not easily get tired while standing. Many other animals relax, rest, and even sleep in their natural standing-up position. We can deduce that the upright posture was forced on humans from the fact that it has brought with it extra fatigue, discomfort and new illnesses, such as curvature of the spine, kidney troubles, back pains, and varicose veins.

The Consequences of the Erect Posture

The upright posture of the human body gave humans a new shape, the result of the redistribution of fat. During the quadripedal locomotion of humans, fat was concentrated on the backs of both male and females, and around the necks of the females. With the gradual adoption of the upright posture the fat, for reasons of balance, slipped down the spine where it remained, forming the buttocks. Buttocks are a peculiar characteristic of the human species.

I explained earlier that when humans gained excess fat in the savannah the females acquired nearly twice that of the males. Most of this extra fat was originally concentrated around the neck, stomach, and thighs. When the human female stood up, the neck fat gradually descended down the front of her body and balanced her buttocks, which were larger than those of the males. Breasts in women and buttocks in both men and women were the humans' balancing factors in their new unnatural and highly precarious position, where the minimal weight not symmetrically distributed and balanced could have upset the stability of the body, knocking its center of gravity off center.

In his book *The Naked Ape* Desmond Morris's explanation of the appearance of women's breasts runs as follows: "If the female of our species was going to successfully shift the interest of the male round to the front, evolution would have to do something to make the frontal region more stimulating" . . . Morris goes on to say that . . . "With the upright posture, a frontal mating came to be adopted, and this created the need to bring sexual signals on to the front of women's bodies as well" . . . He continues: . . . "Can we, if we look at the frontal regions of the female of our species, see any structures that might possibly be mimics of the ancient genital display of hemispherical buttocks and red labia" . . . "The protuberant, hemispherical breasts of the female must surely be copies of the fleshy buttocks, and the sharply defined red lips around the mouth must be copies of the red labia" . . .

I cannot believe that the breasts and buttocks of the human female had anything to do with sexual attraction. If woman had never acquired them, man would still have had the same desire to copulate, as he did in the woodlands and for so many millions of years in the savannah before becoming upright. Besides, humans have sexual intercourse with animals, and animals have neither breasts nor buttocks.

The upright posture, as a result of the demands of gravity, brought some changes in blood pressure and circulation. In the new body position, circulation of blood to the new brain (the brain that was the very cause of bipedalism) became more difficult. As one is aware of the presence of any organ only when it is causing discomfort, so man became aware of his new brain when the circulation of blood to it became more difficult. Thus to this quirk of nature do we owe our self-awareness, self-consciousness, our ability to think abstractly, and our dualism. In this way we can explain the detachment, disconnection, and independence of the mind. In this way we can explain our awareness of the dissociation between mind and body. A synchronized organism, an organism in harmony, an organism in perfect functional integrity, can never be aware of itself.

The sensitivity of the human new brain to changes in blood supply can be deduced by the fact that even a slight diminution in this supply, caused by drugs, malnutrition, or change in the quality of air or rhythm of breathing, can create an extreme dissociation of mind from body, such as trance, hallucination, or fainting.

Another characteristic of humans is their proboscid nose, its purpose being one of the other mysteries in the history of human evolution. It may have been another balancing factor in the human body, particularly for the skull, which took on a new shape with the upright posture. If you look at someone who has just had his nose shortened by surgery you may notice that his posture changes slightly while he gets reaccustomed to the new balance of his head.

Right-handedness

Oakley attributes the reason for right-handedness to the use of tools and weapons by the right hand. This is rather a naïve explanation because surely, before picking up a tool, there must have been a reason for choosing the right hand to do so in preference to the left.

It is more feasible that right-handedness started early in the savannah, when humans walked tripedally, using their right hand to carry extra food. The right side of the body is fractionally heavier than the left, from embryo on, and this unconsciously gave humans more confidence; they felt it was more solid: they felt their right hand was stronger. The right side of the body inspired confidence too, because the temperature on the right of the body is slightly higher than on the left, and in most dual organs such as breasts, thyroids, ovaries, lungs, and testicles, the right ones are more developed than the left.

Above all, given the position of the heart, the left blood vessel which supplies the left hemisphere of the brain where the co-ordinating centers for the right side of the body lie, is shorter, therefore supplying the blood quicker, providing better co-ordination on the right side of the body.

Man the Tool-maker

The majority of writers maintain that by the beginning of the Pleistocene epoch one million years ago, humans took an important step forward—they started making their own tools.

"Miocene and early Pliocene ancestors may have been tool-users without having reached the stage of systematic tool-making," writes K. P. Oakley, in his book *Man the Tool-maker*. In his opinion, by the beginning of the Pleistocene, man was making his own tools.

My contention is that humans did not make their own tools before they reached the stage of Homo sapiens, before they were capable of abstract thoughts. There is no positive evidence that any of the tools exhibited in various museums and attributed to the period before Homo sapiens is a man-made instrument. All objects shown in museums or reproduced in books as artefacts of humans, could have been molded by the elements, objects that could be found shaped by nature today.

The so-called "hand-axes," which would have brought mankind to the so-called period of "hand-ax culture" could have been found at any time near any rocks. Similar sharp objects must have been picked up and used even by the apes, as they do today when they need them.

It is logical that the stone objects attributed to human manufacture before the appearance of Homo sapiens cannot have been made by humans. It is logical because in order to make a tool one needs a tool-making machine or instrument. In order to have a tool-making instrument one needs a developed brain, a brain capable of abstract thoughts. Men could not have imitated other animals in making tools or tool-making instruments, as even today there is no such animal. However conceited humanity may be, we have no positive evidence of any abstract thought before Homo sapiens. Only with the appearance of Homo sapiens can we add to perceptual thinking, which other animals are also capable of, that peculiarity of humans, abstract thinking. Tool-making or weapon-making presupposes holding tools and carrying weapons. This, apart from being an encumbrance to the still precarious upright posture of humans would have contradicted the nature of an opportunist. It may be said that the only pattern of behavior in the life of an opportunist is improvisation, improvisation inspired by the particular objective circumstances at a

"Humans were using stones, bones, and sticks as tools or weapons . . ." An animal bone from the Neolithic period.

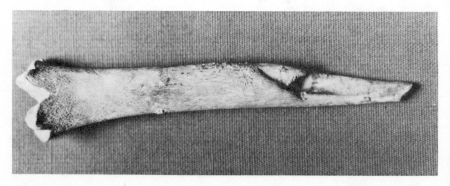

given moment. An improviser never carries tools or weapons, for he never knows what the next situation may be. He gathers his tools and his weapons on the spot, his choice depending on the exigencies of the situation. Carrying tools and weapons presupposes premeditation, which, being abstract thinking, cannot have started before the appearance of Homo sapiens. Before Homo sapiens, humans were not, surely, tool-makers, but tool-gatherers. Humans were using stones, bones, and sticks as tools or weapons, all of which were available for immediate use.

An ape, even today, uses a fallen branch as a tool or weapon, but would never deliberately, even if circumstances demanded it, return to the tree to break off a branch and make it into a stick. This would be a creative mental operation which apes of today and humans of yesterday were incapable of doing.

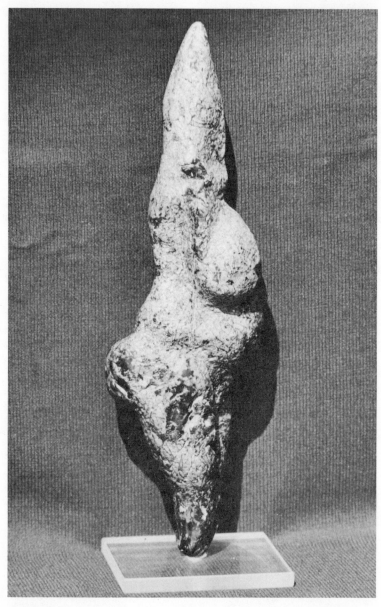

"One of the oldest known statuettes . . . is of a fat and potent-looking lady."

PART TWO

The Adolescent Revolution

Why do we calculate that the beginning of Homo sapiens was during the Upper Paleolithic period? Because in that period we find the first signs of the mind's activity, in the form of art. One of the oldest known statuettes, "Venus of Laussel," a low relief carved on a block of limestone, is of a fat and potent-looking lady, and can be dated at around 27,000 years ago. A woman's torso, carved in hematite and 25,000 years old, was found in Ostrva Petrkovice in Czechoslovakia. Animals carved from stone and ivory 20,000 years ago were found at Württemberg, and a famous limestone statuette of a woman, 18,000 years old, was found in Willendorf in Austria. Around 15–16,000 years ago there were cave paintings.

Earlier than this art, there is no positive evidence of creative thought. How can we deduce this? One of the best definitions of art is still that of Aristotle. To him, "art is a capacity to make, involving a true course of thinking." Making, therefore, involves abstract thinking and there were no man-made objects before 27,000 years ago that "involved a true course of thinking."

We are talking about the mind and its creativity. But how did man discover the mind and its creativity?

When man became aware of the existence of his brain, he confronted it in the way he had faced anything new for millions of years. He played with it. The mind is the result of man playing with his brain.

The first sculptures and paintings were the outcome of the artists playing with their imagination. This is best illustrated in the paintings representing imaginary creatures, parts of various animals muddled together.

In the beginning, art was exploratory play. With the advance of the mind, play became a purposeful game. In this purposeful game art became symbolic, religious, magic or commercial. These were all open means for man to show off his superiority. With his mind, man entered the adolescent phase, the phase of competition.

Scientists disagree about the real meaning of the first known human art. For some it was an "art for art's sake"; for others a kind of "sympathetic magic and totemism." Many scientists feel that the first human art was a "fertility magic." Most of these speculations are based on the theory of so-called "ethnographic parallels," which means comparing the first human artist with those of present-day "primitives"—today's Australian aborigines, for example. This does not help very much, because today's "primitives," however primitive they may appear to the sophisticated observer, have a highly developed culture of their own.

If the first human art was "sympathetic magic and totemism,"

"The first sculptures and paintings were the outcome of the artists playing with their imagination."

"Around 15–16,000 years ago there were cave paintings."

the figures represented would have been symbolic, and therefore stylized, and would not have exhibited a visual realism. Earlier cave art, and also the first statuettes, were representational art; it reproduced impressive images perceived from nature. Later, when humans developed their abstract ideas, more stylized representations were found, as in the figures of hunters in the Valtorta cave, and the "Women danse" from the Cogul cave. Both these paintings are from the Mesolithic period.

Later still the dissolution of figures representing abstract ideas reached extremes and became character symbols. This symbolic representation in paintings and engravings inspired Sumerian pictographic writing in the fourth millennium B.C.

The interpretation of the first human cave art as "fertility magic" can be disputed, for it was executed earlier than any notions of fertility. The notion of fertility developed around the eighth millennium B.C., with the first agricultural and the domestication of animals. It was then that the survival of the human species started depending on fertility. Of woman's fertility, men could not possibly have any notion, let alone have given it any importance. There are no indisputable sexual signs or symbols, nor scenes of copulation of any kind in the whole of Paleolithic art.

The interpretation "art for art's sake" cannot be very compelling either. If the first human painters had been capable of appreciating art for art's sake, surely there would be evidence that their minds had developed at a much earlier stage.

The fact that generation after generation painted over the same walls on top of existing paintings, contributes to the difficulty of interpreting the real meaning of the first human art.

In judging our first painters, scientists tend to attribute their own patterns of thought to them. We cannot attribute what the French like to call *spiritualité* to the mind at its dawn, when *spiritualité* was reached by the mind, thousands of years later.

Any artist, at the beginning of his artistic life and in his first work, finds himself in the same situation as the first human artist. With his first work, the first human artist wanted to impress, to realize an effect and to inspire admiration, admiration which implied his superiority.

What impressed others?

"What impresses me, helps me impress others," the artist says to himself. "Impressing others will put me in a superior position. If I am impressed by the aggression of a bull or the speed of a horse, I will impress my audience if I succeed in reproducing them." This was the simple reasoning of our first artists. Most of the cave paintings represented very impressive animals such as bison, horses, oxen, and mammoths. There were no landscapes, or

". . . the figures in the Valtorta cave . . ."

paintings of trees and plants, lakes or rivers. The primitive humans were clearly not impressed by them, as they were part of their life. Paintings of birds were seldom found in the cave paintings, and hyenas never. There were also surprisingly few paintings of food animals, such as antelope, sheep, and goat, and also very few of man himself and of his first friend, the dog.

Impressive animals were usually depicted in an impressive manner, like bisons, the black painted stag with outstanding antlers, the black painted bull, horses and the "jumping cow," all from the Lascaux cave, or the red painted elephant in the El Castillo cave, the engraved bison in the La Greze cave, and the dying

"If I am impressed by the aggression of a bull or the speed of a horse, I will impress my audience if I succeed in reproducing them."

bison, the wild boar ready to charge in the Altamira cave. The look on the face of the savage cat in the Combarelles cave frightens visitors even today.

That the aim of the first artists was to impress can be deduced also from the representation of imaginary creatures such as the famous "Sorcerer" in Les Trois Frères cave.

What is the connection between an image in the mind and its exteriorization?

Any abstract idea craves to become reality. Impressed by his own abstract thought, an artist falls in love with it. It is his personal achievement and he has the urge to display it. He is in search of admiration which will give him the feeling of sufficiency, of completeness.

From the first human painters to modern adolescents, the story is the same—all like to show off their impressions. It makes them feel more important and less alone. Most adolescents, at the beginning of the abstract creativity of their mind, start a "journal" or diary in which they note their first impressions. Cave paintings, the "journal" of any adolescent, or the carving of initials on a tree or monument, have much in common.

Writers interpreting cave art as "sympathetic magic and totemism" or "fertility magic," or as "art for art's sake," did not study the drawings and inscriptions of adolescents on the walls of public lavatories all over the world, or the drawings and inscriptions of adolescents on the carriages of subways and buses in New York City. There they would find much in common with cave paintings. An American adolescent explained his "art" on the sides of subway carriages, in an interview with the New York *Times.* "I have carved my name all around. There ain't nowhere I go I can't see it. I sometimes go on Sunday to 7th Avenue and 86th Street station and just spend the whole day watching my name go by."

From the following historical text written by an Egyptian artist from the twentieth century b.c., we have an idea of the superior feelings of our first artists. "I was an artist, skilled in my art, excellent in my learning . . . I knew how to render the movements of a man and the carriage of a woman . . . and the speed of a runner. No one succeeds in all these things save only myself and the eldest son of my body."

Cave paintings have a strange characteristic and a certain mystery. The caves in which paintings were discovered were all inaccessible and dark. One has the impression that the first human art was painted in secret places.

At the beginning of the working of his mind, an adolescent will hide in caves or places protected from open spaces in order to find himself. Man could have started building a roof as much for psychological reasons, feelings of agoraphobia, as for climatic reasons. At the beginning of the working of his mind, an adolescent is frightened by the omnipotence of it, of its wilderness. Later, when the adolescent discovered the power of his mind and the power of beliefs, he invented gods, to protect him from the open spaces, the main characteristics of gods' being, in fact, their omnipresence. Whenever man becomes disillusioned by his gods he goes to the open spaces, into the wilderness, in search of new gods.

When man discovered his capacity for reproducing his impressions plastically, he obviously reproduced what impressed him most.

What was among man's first impressions when he became aware of his brain and of himself? Authority, the mother. Man was still a dependent being. He was not impressed by any particular woman, as the heads and faces of the statuettes were only indicated, never elaborated. It was women in general that impressed him, their authority, their solidity.

When the human male crosses the bridge into adolescence, he burns it, thus cutting the umbilical cord with the mother, the authority and organization which helped him to reach adolescence. He wants autonomy, he wants independence. The scars on his old brain engraved with our first fathers' separation in search of autonomy and independence, start to itch when man reaches adolescence. In any adolescent there is a Brutus trying to achieve his freedom by breaking with his Caesar. Brutus, Saint-Just rightly observed, had to kill Caesar, or kill himself. Marduk, in the first epic of creation of old Babylon, in order to become god, had to kill his mother.

How does male humanity achieve autonomy?

Rebellion! All rebellions and revolutions have one thing in

"He was not impressed by any particular woman, as the heads and faces of the statuettes were only indicated, never elaborated."

common. They all aim for autonomy, liberation from the hierarchy, freedom from the past.

Autonomy is always fought for in the name of liberty, but once autonomy becomes established, the first thing that perishes is liberty. Violence and terror are the first stages in any adolescent autonomy. In this stage we have a new hierarchical order and new values which bring with them the seeds of a new rebellion, and so on. All rebellions of the human species are the same.

Here is the description of the first recorded rebellion by mankind. The quotations are from *Admonitions* by the sage Egyptian Ipuwer, written some forty-one centuries ago. "The King has been removed by the populace" . . . "The archives are destroyed, public offices are violated" . . . "The officials are murdered" . . . "A man takes his shield when he goes to plough. A man smites his brother, his mother's son" . . . "The poor man is full of joy" . . . "Gold is hoarded" . . . "The robber has riches, boxes of ebony are smashed. Precious acacia wood is cleft assunder" . . . "Every town says: 'Let us suppress the powerful among us'" . . . "She who looked at her face in the water is now the owner of a mirror" . . . "All female slaves are free with their tongues" . . . "The owners of robes are now in rags" . . . "Serfs have become the owners of serfs."

As Hegel rightly said: "What experience and history teach us is that people and governments have never learnt anything from history, or acted on principles deduced from it."

Going back to our first artists, in their first creativity phase they wanted to please the authority. As soon as they attained full adolescence, however, their aim was to impress their fellow adolescents. Adolescence is a phase of competition and antagonism.

The adolescent era also brought with it the characteristics of adolescence: envy and jealousy. The superiority of some was the inferiority of the others, which created envy, jealousy, suspicion, and tension. Fellow men will accept another man's superiority and leadership only if through this superiority they can achieve their own purpose, to be superior in some way as well.

What purpose did the first human male adolescents have in common? It was rebellion against woman and her domination. The barely accessible dark caves soon became the hiding place of the adolescents. There the first gang was born. From this primitive adolescent gang, gathering in the secrecy of a cave, to the cardinals of today meeting in a conclave, there is little difference.

With gangs, secrecy and conspiracy were born, the life blood of gangs. The hidden, dark cave suited the human male, frightened of being found out by the dominating mother and derided for his self-infatuation.

Through the cave meetings and cave paintings of our primitive ancestors, human males acquired new identities: the togetherness and solidarity of those in possession of a secret. Joining the gang, man entered into the role imposed by the gang, and an important feeling was born, a feeling of loyalty, loyalty to the common cause.

That the caves were places of initiation to a gang can be deduced by the considerable number of painted hands. On the walls of the El Castillo and Gargas caves there are about 182 paintings of hands, some crippled, some with missing fingers. In at least twenty other caves in France, Spain, and Italy, there are paintings of human hands.

Three facts emerge from these paintings. First, painting a hand is simple as one places it flat on the wall and traces round it, in and out of the fingers. This was the easiest initiation. Secondly, as most of the hands depicted were either mutilated or deformed, the caves must have been meeting places for the rejected humans living on the edge of the groups. There was no pity in premind human society. Physical abnormality was either rejected or feared as a freak of nature. The third fact proves that Paleolithic man was mainly right-handed. In the El Castillo and Gargas caves 159 were left hands and only 23 were right ones.

S. Giedion, a scientist who studied the meaning of the hands in the cave paintings, in his *The Eternal Present*, writes: "The cloud of mutilated hands at Gargas stands there like a tragic chorus eternally crying out for help and mercy." This passage proves that scientists judge the past in the light of their own prejudices, their own religious ideas. Mercy and charity developed much later, and only as an expedient of the mind. In the Roman salute of the first Nazi gangs, and in the revolutionary salute of the first anarchist gangs, many mutilated hands would have been evident, and they were certainly not pleading for mercy.

With adolescence the human male acquires another peculiarity: secrecy. In secrecy man feels protected from the outside world which might deride or challenge his self-created image of himself. In secrecy he feels safe in his own world of self-importance. Secrecy is the food of conceit.

Human male civilization was started by a gang in a cave, by a gang rebelling against an establishment, an order. Human male civilization, up until modern times, has never been anything but a civilization of gangs. The human male is lost without a gang. A gang is a substitute for the mother.

The first gang mentioned in history was the Babylonian "horde" from the Sumero-Akkadian *Epic of Creation*. The word "horde" was more appropriate in context with this epic, because the first organized adolescent rebels in Babylonia came mostly from the pastoral element. When the Goddess Tiamat gave her husband the "tables of destinies," the symbols of power, to encourage him in the war against the young gods, she said: "Your word will hold the rebel horde."

In essence there is no difference between the first gang of human males and the gangs of Napoleon and Hitler; no difference between Pericles' gang in the fifth century B.C., the Borgias in the fifteenth century or Christ's gang of the twelve apostles; no difference between the gang in White's Club, London, or a gang of Puerto Ricans on the West Side of New York City. All political parties and social classes are based on the mentality of the gang.

Two great writers of sociology, Mosca and Pareto call governing gangs "elites" or "ruling classes."

Webster's dictionary gives the following definition of a gang: "A group of persons drawn together by a community of tastes, interests or activity." In this definition of the word one can see its origin and the characteristics of its components. What kind of a being needs a gang to achieve more than he could alone? Only a frightened and insufficient being; these are characteristics of the human male.

Ever since the first human adolescent revolution, up until the present day there is one gang stronger than the rest. This gang will always impose its "tastes, interests and activities" on the others. The more irrational the ideas and tastes, the more aggressive the gang, and the more aggressive the gang, the more successful it becomes. The history of mankind is a continuing example of this human logic. John Plamenatz, in his *Democracy and Illusion*, rightly stressed that it is not the rational side of religions or ideologies which appeals to the masses, but the irrational side. "Conscious and unconscious rebellion against the rational, respect given to Id at the expenses of ego, are hallmarks of our times," explains J. Monod in his *Chance and Necessity*. One thing I could add is that it was not the hallmarks of "our times," but that it has been the same ever since the beginning of the first adolescent revolution.

One cannot but smile at the paradoxical mentality of mankind reading and rereading the following words of Goethe: "It is the greatest joy of the man of thought, to have explored the explorable and then calmly to revere the inexplorable."

All gangs are aggressive. Aggression in an individual is caused by an individual mind and its idea of superiority. Jung, spurred on by Freud's individual unconsciousness, invented a collective one. I stress "invented," because no such thing exists in reality. In any gang there is a collective mind with a clear and positive idea of superiority. The Nazi gang was not guided by any "un-consciousness," but by a clear idea of superiority, the idea of *Übermensch.* The Nazis even gave scientific descriptions of "in-ferior-man," man to be eliminated. This was not a collective un-consciousness but a perfectly clear belief. The British gang of East India Trade robbed and exploited India, not in the name of "unconsciousness," but in the name of real interest inspired by two beliefs: belief in mercantilism and belief in British superiority.

Today everyone is scandalized by the activities of some young criminal gangs, robbing and destroying other people's property, but no one objects when the political party in power gives the responsible jobs in national economy to their incompetent or dis-honest fellow believers, to the members of their gang.

In the Vatican, during the war, there were newspapers from countries all over the world. The German and Italian press called Roosevelt, "the leader of the Judeo-Masonic gang," Churchill, the leader of the "plutocratic and imperialistic gang," and Stalin, the leader of the "Asian, barbarian Communist gang." The Allied press referred to the German government as the "Nazi gang," and to the Italian government as the "Fascist gang."

The secret of a gang's success is secrecy. Karl Marx was right when he discovered that the purpose of secrecy was "mystifica-tion" on which any hierarchical system or any superiority leans.

Adolescents need to show off their secrecy to others in order to impress them with the superiority of belonging to a group. How did adolescents solve this problem of showing off a secret?

By inventing auto-decoration.

The most usual auto-decorations of humans are: tattooing, scarification, circumcision, hair styles, beards and mustaches, ties, badges, epaulettes, blazers and lately, jeans. There is little difference between Indian war paint, African tattoos, the Old Etonian tie, a Sicilian mafioso's sideburns, a teddy boy's leather jacket, and a cardinal's hat.

Justinian, confronted with the Nika Riot, followed the wise advice of his wife, Theodora. She knew the psychology of men and advised him to put on his imperial robes before presenting himself to the masses. "The purple is a glorious winding-sheet," she insisted.

From the ancient Huns to the Heidelberg students, men have tried to modify their looks in order to impress.

Some scientists claim that decoration is inherent in human nature; that it is an instinct. In my view, decoration is not inherent in human nature. It has been copied from animals. Animals display their innate bodily "aggressive signals," to impress.

That auto-decoration is not an instinct can be shown by the fact that all the human male's display signals are not innate but man-made signals, varying from culture to culture. The meaning of the display of decoration in the animal world, copied by the human male, is to impress, therefore to subdue, to subjugate the opponent. To an adolescent everyone is an opponent except the members of his own gang.

The human female also used, and still uses, auto-decoration. Unlike the male however, her intention is to seduce by pleasing, not to subdue by impressing.

Man's urge to permanently display decoration only proves that he is living in a permanent state of anxiety. An animal only displays his aggressive signals when frightened, when trying to impress.

The next step in auto-decoration was masquerading. This starts when man assumes a supernatural role. We have evidence that this pretentious behavior started in the Paleolithic epoch, soon after the mind began to feel self-confidence. By looking at the so-called "imaginary creatures" or the "fantastic beings," such as the "Sorcerer" in the Les Trois Frères cave, the "Dancer," with the bear head in the Le Mas d'Azil cave, and many creatures half animal, half man, we see man's desire to be supernatural.

Ceremonies and rituals started the decoration of the gang's collective ideas. From the ceremonies of the first gang, and those performed in the middle ages, to rituals in the Vatican and the Kremlin, there is little difference. They are all the same game, a decoration of the gang's beliefs, with the purpose of impressing.

What is the ultimate aim of impressing by ceremonies and rituals?

It is to achieve the subtlest of conquests: reverence, genuflection. Ceremonies and rituals are the life blood of collective beliefs.

One of the gods of the Vedic Pantheon, in 1500 B.C., was Agni, the god of ceremonies. The first hymn of Rig-Veda opens with the following verse: "I laud Agni the chosen priest, God, minister of sacrifice" . . .

K'ung, in the sixth century B.C., established ceremonies on all levels of Chinese life.

Perfumes are another achievement of humans, realized through the imitation of animals, who use their natural scent to impress, to please, or to seduce. Humans have used perfumes since prehistoric times. From the beginning of organized religions, perfumes, especially myrrh, were used in temples in order to create a seductive atmosphere. In ancient Egypt each god had his own "fragrance."

Most writers explain that at some point man became aware of the existence of his brain and started using it in a different way. They do not explain when and how it happened, however, or what man's first thoughts and his methods of thinking were.

The brain is the center of mental activity in both animals and humans. The most important mental activities are memory, intelligence intended as the power to understand objective reality, reasoning intended as the use of intelligence within the limits of the laws of nature, and the activity of abstract thought. The first three mental activities can be performed by some animals, but abstract thought can only be exercised by men.

How did man achieve this ability?

How and why did man begin using his brain for an independent activity? What happened?

The brain is like puberty: at a certain stage it starts to itch.

I have already stated that when man became aware of his brain, he faced it with the only activities that he knew: curiosity, play, and exploration. From playing with his brain he discovered abstract thought. Abstract thoughts are, therefore, the product of man's playing with his brain, an activity he may have discovered by analogy to sexual masturbation.

One of the first-known myths of creation, the old Egyptian myth, gives us an idea of the early working of the mind. When the Atum-Re discovered his mind, the Heliopolis myth explains, then he "who came into being of himself," created everything else: the universe, the visible and the invisible, the known and unknown. The god created the external world, as any adolescent creates his world, after his own image, his self-created image. "I planned in my heart how I should make every shape," stated the old Egyptian god.

How did the god create every shape?

"He put his penis in his hand for the pleasure of emission," explains the myth, "and there were born brother and sister" . . . From this "brother and sister" came the whole Egyptian pantheon of gods followed by man and woman.

In the Sumerian *Enke and the World Order* it is explained how their god of waters created Tigris, on which the life of the Sumerians depended. "He lifts his penis, ejaculates, thus filling the Tigris with sparkling waters."

Why did man take so long to discover his brain and to become aware of its existence?

There is evidence that 150–200,000 years ago the human brain was the same volume as that of Homo sapiens. Why then, did man only start using it for abstract reasoning about 30,000 years ago?

Curiosity and exploratory play are stronger in infants than memory. A child will play with the same toy over and over again if there is nothing more interesting to do. He has a memory but he does not trust it. A memory has no realistic meaning for him. It does not lean on anything which can give him confidence. Use of memory would be in contrast with an infant's nature; it would prevent playing and exploring. Without the use of memory there is no real abstract mental activity.

What was it then, that urged man to use his memory?

It was a sudden self-confidence which he acquired when, by playing with his brain he realized that he could produce wishful thoughts. No one really knows when man started playing with his brain, but we know that his first abstract thoughts came about 30,000 years ago. It was with this self-confidence that the era of adolescence started.

One of the first methods of thinking in order to reach abstract thought must have been analogy. This analogy at the beginning of man's abstract mental activity was of syllogistic character. There is evidence of this syllogistic reasoning in some of the Upper Paleolithic burial caves. Before the mind was discovered our ancestors had no idea of death. In these caves our ancestors coated their dead with red ochre. For them blood was a sign of life, blood was red, therefore red signified the source of life. We can find this kind of thinking today in some forms of schizophrenic, archaic reasoning.

Man made yet another discovery while playing with his brain. He discovered the idea of truth, an important discovery for a creature with no innate pattern of behavior. Truth became the ' repetition of natural events. Heraclitus understood this when he said: "It follows that the coming-to-be of anything, if it is absolutely necessary, must be cyclical—i.e. must return upon itself."

With the development of the mind, alas, man discovered what Plato called "useful lies." The human mind, realizing that truth was the repetition of an event, succeeded to fool itself by the artificial or verbal repetition of useful lies, thus transforming them into truths. Political and religious propaganda is based on this syllogism. This syllogism produced the mind's damaging invention—rhetoric.

What is an abstract idea, and how did man achieve it?

An abstract idea is nothing but the wishful thinking of an incomplete being concerning the unknown, the unexplored, or the inexplorable. The ancient Egyptians were right when they placed the source of the mind in the heart. Wishful thinking soon became a belief on which man could lean in order to find peace when confronted with the unexplored. The unexplored had to be explained through wishful thinking or wishful belief, otherwise man could not enjoy the explored. He would be too frightened.

Man, being an opportunist in permanent search of a better adaptation, is an explorer by nature. An explorer will always be attracted to the unexplored.

Why?

There is only one way a curious and incomplete being sees the unexplored: optimistically, hopefully, wishfully.

When the brain discovered the mind, or its capacity for creating abstract thoughts or wishful thinking, it became so proud of it that it became a slave to it. It is the nature of the creation to enslave the creator.

What happened to the other activity of the brain, its intelligence, intelligence intended as the understanding of nature and its laws? The brain's intelligence became a blind servant of the mind's creation, belief. Man started seeing nature with eyes focused by the mind. Reality became "ought to be reality."

In discovering its power to create abstract thoughts, the mind started flirting with itself, worshiping itself. Man succeeded where no animal would ever succeed—to flatter himself and, what is more, to believe in his own flattery. Why?

The answer is that any abstract thinking is always wishful thinking.

Fascinated by the power of his mind and unhappy with his un-natural environment and his position in it, man started creating an abstract environment to suit himself, or rather his wishful image of himself. In his transcendental world man imagined him-self the way he thought he should be as a complete being.

With the mind man discovered a new pleasure, the pleasure of his mind. This pleasure became the main drive of the human male's behavior. Even sexual and sensual pleasures became subor-dinated to the pleasure of the mind. Fervent believers are seldom interested in the pleasures of sex.

What is this power of the mind?

It is the ability to create ideas about oneself and the world. But ideas cannot exist by themselves, they need help. Passion and love were added to the adolescent mind's creation, the idea. Only man can love, only man can have illusions. What we call the love of children is nothing but a biological comfort. What we call love of women for men is nothing but a biological, mental, and finan-cial comfort, or an adaptation to the new element in the environ-ment, man's love of his ideas. A woman's attitude towards her children is dictated by her maternal instinct, which stems from concern for the good of the progeny. Lacking a maternal in-stinct, a woman imitates man and develops love for her children which, in essence, is love for herself, her psychological, biological, or social comforts. It has nothing to do with the good of the progeny.

The only possible love is the love of an idea, of an abstract cre-ation. The idea can only survive if leaning on love; it has no nat-ural roots. Love, too, being an abstract phenomenon has to lean on something. It invents beliefs. Love, in order to exist, has to blind itself by beliefs. A belief is the guardian of blindness, the protector of ideas from their enemy, objective reality. Belief becomes a defender of the supernatural against the natural. But belief, too, has to lean on something to exist. It finds its strength in its own invention, in arrogance. Beliefs put their creator in artificially superior positions, positions which have to be defended. In arrogance, this protective shield of the supernatural, lies the origin of a unique aggression in nature. We will call this man-made aggression, a believer's aggression. The source of man's aggression lies in his mind.

"Love and do what you want," said St. Augustine, meaning, presumably, religious love, the love of an idea. In the name of the love of Jesus, Christians have committed numerous crimes. The main evil deeds are not committed out of hatred but out of love, the love of an idea. Only a believer can be evil. Solzhenitsyn was right when he said: "To do evil a human being first of all must believe that what he is doing is good."

Aggression started with the mind. Aggression is the use of physical strength in defending an abstract world against enemies. The enemies of beliefs, from the first believer to Stalin, are always the same. They are non-believers in their own beliefs. "Who is not with me is against me," is the motto of all believers. The adolescent era is the era of partisans. Only a partisan of Christ can conceive the idea of an anti-Christ.

Humanity, ever since it entered the phase of beliefs, has not changed regarding the extermination of opponents, the infidels or the other side. From Sumerian or Egyptian believers to contemporary believers, there has been no difference in dealing with the enemy. Here I quote a description of an Egyptian historian and general, Weni, of 4,400 years ago, about his punitive expedition against his enemies, against non-believers, non-believers in Egyptian superiority. He calls his enemies by the denigrating name of "sand-dwellers." He wrote:

> The army returned in peace, it had cut down
> Its figs and wines.
> This army returned in peace, it had cast fire
> Into all its princely houses.
> This army returned in peace, it had slain troops
> In many tens of thousands.

This army returned in peace, it had carried away
Many troops as prisoners.
And his Majesty praised me on account of it more than
   anything.

The use of physical violence in defending or imposing beliefs
has not changed since the first believer right up to the modern
extremists. The former used his muscles, the latter knives, guns,
or bombs.

In play, a child or a man in infancy is an instrument of his play.
He is his own toy, he is his own train, his own horse, etc. He is a
third person. With the discovery of the mind, a human male
enters the adolescent phase, he enters into the first person.

With his mind man saw himself, or more accurately, he
created himself. Until then, like any other animal, he only knew
the outside world, the universe without him. When man created
himself he fell in love with himself, he became the universe, the
center of the universe. With the mind, man assumed a role, a
role given to him by his own mind. He abandoned childish play
and entered into a game, the game of roles. Life became a theater.
Men started acting life instead of living it. Only a being living a
life of roles could have had the idea of writing for the stage.

The women and children accepted this new way of life, the
women by adapting themselves, by imitating the game of roles,
and the children by playing with them. In the theatrical life of an
adolescent there are two main characters: man in the role of Don
Quixote, woman in the role of Sancho Panza. Ortega y Gasset
was right when he wrote: "The woman goes to the theatre; the
man carries it inside himself and is the impresario of his own
life."

Assumed roles imposed by abstract beliefs need affirmation.
Adolescents soon create competition. They think it gives life to
the assumed roles. Competition is an absurdity in the life of an
opportunist. The nature of an opportunist needs collaboration
and consensus. In modern history, competition is considered an
economic value. But in logical terms competition is the destruction of resources. There is no competition which can produce
more than co-operation.

Competition is in the nature of adolescents. Competition produces victims, and the human male needs victims to feel self-confident, to feel superior. Men, or gangs of men, will always invent and impose the game in which they excel, giving themselves a better chance of winning.

What is the real aim of a game, this invention of man in his adolescent phase? Do games produce victories or victor? From the point of view of natural logic, a game cannot produce victory, only a victor. Who then is the victor? The victor is whoever provides a loser, the loser being proof of the victor's superiority. The only positive realization of games, activities of competition and antagonism are, therefore, losers.

Huizinga was inaccurate when he said that play was an irrational activity. It is games that are the irrational activities.

Man discovered the power of his mind and the power of self-infatuation. These powers inspired arrogance in him and the audacity to use his physical strength. Before Homo sapiens, the use of physical strength was not practiced by humans. We do not know if man, before becoming sapiens was stronger than woman, but his audacity in using his physical strength put him a position to be stronger than woman. Woman's instinct of adaptation helped him.

The audacity of man is unique. The word comes from the Latin *audere*, meaning to dare, to defy laws and rules. What animal could defy the rules of nature? Only an incomplete animal, an animal without innate rules, without an innate pattern of behavior, only an animal who had nothing to lose, an animal able to invent "*Après moi le déluge*" would dare to be audacious. Man started breaking the pattern of life based on woman's natural superiority, a pattern that had existed for millions of years.

The adolescent revolution introduced a radical change in sexual relationships. Instead of being seduced by the female, therefore reduced to the position of a pleasing slave, an obedient servant, the male wanted to seduce. He wanted to reduce woman to his slave and servant.

But what were his means of seduction?

Seduction presupposes superiority. What was this superiority? Man's only superiority over woman was his readiness to use his physical strength. He perpetrated the first incongruity of his new life, he used force and violence to seduce. He substituted woman's promiscuity with his own. The more women he had sexual intercourse with, the more powerful he felt. Man became obsessed with virility. The cult of the bull was born at the dawn of man's adolescent revolution, and the bull, the symbol of "genetic strength" became a sacred animal to man. From the Upper Paleolithic cave paintings, and the sculptures of the Çatal Hüyük shrines of the seventh millennium b.c., to the figurines of Starčevo and Vinča of the fifth millennium b.c., bulls are a prominent feature in art.

"Many Greeks reproduce Dionysus' image in the form of a bull," stressed Plutarch. Even Zeus transformed himself into a bull in order to seduce Europa.

The following passage from the *Iliad* shows Zeus extolling his virility on seducing Hera: "Today let us enjoy the delights of love. Never has such desire, for goddess or woman flooded and overwhelmed my heart; not even when I loved Ixion's wife, who bore Pirithous to rival the gods in wisdom; or Danae of the slim ankles, the daughter of Aerisius who gave birth to Perseus, the greatest hero of his time; or the far-famed daughter of Phoenix, who bore me Minos and the godlike Rhadamanthus; or Semele, or Alemene in Thebes whose son was the lion-hearted Heracles, while Semele bore Dionysus to give pleasure to Mankind; or Demeter, Queen of the lovely locks, or the incomparable Leto; or when I fell in love with you yourself, never have I felt such love, such sweet desire, as fills me now for you."

Man soon realized the difficulty of keeping woman with his virility. He then reduced her to his slave by using moral, religious, legal and economic coercion. Lack of virility was solved by forbidding his woman to have sexual intercourse with anyone but him, punishing her adultery with death. In some Latin countries until very recently, women were killed for adultery.

The promiscuous women who did not wish to conform to the rules imposed on them by men were rejected and often persecuted. They were labeled harlots or other such names of contempt. The following old Babylonian advice is typical of the adolescent male's opinion of female rebels: "Do not marry a harlot whose husbands are 6,000."

Zeus pursuing Semele, mother
of Dionysus.

"Man became obsessed with virility."

"Man invented a mask. . . ."

After his successful adolescent revolution, man wanted to differ physically even more from women. In the drawings, engravings and sculptures of the Indo-European, Sumerian, Assyrian or Greek early history, the first peoples to liberate themselves from women, men are depicted with beards and are dressed differently from women. In places where the adolescent revolution took longer to succeed, the men in the pictures are clean-shaven and dressed in the same way as women. The reason that man was depicted without a beard in female-dominated societies was that either the beard only started to grow when man emerged from his infancy phase, or because man wanted to be similar to woman in appearance.

The mind, putting man in a supernatural position, changed everything. Life, which in nature is a purpose in itself, became for man an instrument for his beliefs. Life became a slave of beliefs. Men started killing themselves and their fellow men and even their own flesh and blood in the name of their beliefs.

How did man reach this absurd situation?

Adolescent humanity was trying to be what, by nature, it was not. The mind invented "ought to be." "That short but imperious word 'ought,' so full of high significance," explained Darwin. Man achieved what no animal or woman will ever achieve: not to be himself, but to become his own wishful thinking. Man became what his mind dictated to him that he ought to be. The "ought to be" became his life in spite of nature, and against nature.

Man's invention of "ought to be" is evidence that he has no "be," that he is not a complete being, that he is a "becoming" being. A becoming being never reaches maturity. Since the invention of "ought to be" the human pattern of behavior started relying on it. Man became his own most obedient servant. From being his own servant to becoming others' servant, from "ought to be" to the categorical imperative of "thou shalt," the step was short.

Man imposes on himself a role in the game of life, a role inspired by his mind. Man invented a mask and put it over his face, over his whole being; the mask represented the "ought." Only man's mind, this creator of "oughts" could have thought up the idea of a mask. The mask pretends to be something or someone else.

Prehistory offers us a variety of artistic representations of masks. The Vinča and Starčevo artists in the sixth millennium B.C. dedicated their skill with particular enthusiasm to sculptural masks.

In several languages, even today, men address each other in the third person as if addressing a mask.

The "ought to be," reflecting a transcendental world, brought man out of the real world. Ever since the mind began to create abstract ideas, no man ever lived in this world; he lived, and still lives in his own world, imprisoned there by his own beliefs.

We may ask if beliefs, those discoveries of male humanity and imposed on the women and children, were any good to the human species and its future.

Beliefs bring aggression, human aggression, the most evil aggression in nature. But what is even more dangerous is that beliefs reduce curiosity and exploration, the most important factors in the life of the human species. In this sense, beliefs become what specializations are for highly specialized animals; both reduce curiosity; both are only interested in what suits their limited fields. Beliefs halt progress, progress toward better harmony with the universe. Belief considers itself perfect. Perfection does not allow for curiosity or exploration. It therefore causes stagnation or regression.

When human males discovered their brain, and through it their mind, and through their mind the idea of superiority, and through this superiority, aggression, they started to use this aggression, not only against their mothers, but against other human groups as well.

Between 20–30,000 years ago, our ancestors began writing the history of Homo sapiens with the blood of the innocent. They suppressed their cousins of the Neanderthal type who were still in infancy. By 20,000 years ago the adolescent gangs of our direct ancestors succeeded in eliminating from the face of the earth, all the lesser-developed human groups. Ever since then the self-assertion of a human group has been at the expense of other groups.

The first adolescent revolution was a slow but gradual process starting with Homo sapiens and going on until approximately the third century A.D. Its main characteristic was rebellion against women and their dominating role in society, in the name of man's abstract thought. With adolescence a new male humanity was born.

Ritualistic ceremonies in many cultures have been performed ever since the beginning of history, and always at the start of the adolescent phase. The meaning of all these ceremonies is always the same; the death of one being and the birth of another; the birth of a new personality which has nothing to do with the dead one. In a number of ancient myths, a boy is swallowed by a monster and then rejected by it, but as a new being, the monster giving to that new being during his transition a new personality, leaving scars or toothmarks on him.

There are many rituals in history indicating the transition from childhood to adolescence, but not one shows us the transition from adolescence to adulthood. In my view, male humanity has never advanced beyond the stage of adolescence.

I am aware that my theory of adolescence as a new phase of life independent of childhood in the human male, will be questioned by many psychiatrists and psychoanalysts. To them childhood is the basis of future man; it explains everything. But so does instinct for sociologists and economists; so does God for the religious; and the palm of the hand for fortunetellers.

But are any of these explanations true?

In my view, many scientists exaggerate in their speculations about childhood. Freud illustrated his preconceived ideas with a number of so-called "clinical examples." But did they really exist or were they invented, invented to suit his metaphysical speculations? Why did Freud and his followers not illustrate the thousands of examples which contradicted his thesis? Freud and his followers suffer, as Bertrand Russell rightly stressed, from Hegelian illusions which in practical terms means that they see in childhood what their abstract preconceived thought needs to see. Perhaps this is why their methods treat the mentally disturbed but do not cure them.

Adolescence, being a phase of beliefs, therefore a phase of

doubts and conversions, has nothing to do with the innocent play and exploration of childhood.

It is not childhood that determines the personality of adolescence. It is playing with the brain, building up the mind which is of essential importance for future life. This starts at the threshold of adolescence. As science has dedicated no efforts to this important period in man's life, the period of the formation of his ideas about himself, no one has ever explained what really happens at this stage. No one really knows how and why, out of a charming and gay boy, a rude and gloomy adolescent suddenly emerges; why a clean and honest child grows into a cheat, a liar, or a thief.

A human adolescent cannot judge or analyze childhood. It is a different world with different values and a different language; one is purposeless exploratory play, the second a purposeful game. Man judges childhood as he judges everything else: by himself, by his own ideas, by his mind. We think our children are aggressive only because we are aggressive. A gangster will see a gangster in every child. A Freudian will find that every child suffers from the Oedipus and other complexes. A sex maniac will see a sex maniac in every child. A perverse or cruel adolescent will claim that a child's exploratory play with animals is perverse or cruel.

Freud, before being a scientist, was an adolescent human being, and the nature of adolescent humanity is to judge everything and everyone, throughout history, by the mind, by preconceptions or metaphysical speculations, in relation to abstract ideas.

That Freud was the prototype of adolescence can be deduced from his gloominess. Adolescence is a gloomy stage.

Helmut Schulze points out that Freud never mentions the word joy in any of his works. Adolescents are only aware of achievements, victories compensated by orgasmic pleasure which leaves them in the well-known post-orgasmic depression.

Childhood, through exploration and play, is a preparation for an opportunistic life. When the child becomes an adolescent, however, he enters an idealistic world in which he obeys a role, he obeys the beliefs of his mind. It is not the childhood experiences which influence his adolescent idea about himself and his romantic place in the world. It is conceit, once formed, that finds its justification or interpretations in childhood. Between the two world wars a large number of British and French upper-class adolescents, with happy, normal backgrounds, chose, out of pure exhibitionism, following an intellectual fashion, to become Communists. They all found justifying experiences for their attitudes from their childhood, because they looked back on this period of their lives with the minds of Communists. Many of these British and French Communists found justifying experiences for their conversion to Catholicism, Humanism, alcoholism, and homosexuality in the same childhood. The repeated conversions of human beings prove that childhood is only a reservoir of experiences to be interpreted, chosen, as the justifying element for changing the mind. Childhood could be compared to a library where one goes to choose the book suited to one's frame of mind at that moment. Looking back on his life, an old man will see how many times his beliefs, loves, etc. have changed. His childhood, however, remains the same one.

Human males in the adolescent phase always find an excuse in their childhood to justify any change of belief. Adolescents cannot live with the feeling of responsibility. If they fail to find their own excuses, psychiatrists will help, and together they will be satisfied in their illusions.

Adolescents do not like to give the impression that they change their beliefs or ideas. Above all they hate to be reminded of their previous beliefs or loves. Adolescents are always suspicious of people who remember.

Childhood bears no relation to the personality of the adolescent, as claimed by psychiatrists of today. This is evident from the first major move the adolescent makes. The adolescent's first step, which makes him "adult" in his mind, is his own independence of mind. He dreams of separation, a separation from the past, an abrupt rupture with the past.

Between infancy and adolescence, there is a third large group of humanity which stops and lives on a bridge between the two. This third group of humans grew out of play and exploration, but never reached the purposeful games or beliefs of adolescents. This group became obsessed by novelty, novelty imposed by propaganda, the fashion or latest trend. Novelty became the purpose. This group lives in the phase of neophilia. Living for novelty gives this sterile humanity a lasting feeling of growing up, of becoming the future. That is how they try to find their identity, their feeling of superiority; the protection of being "with it."

Man's vanity, pretentiousness, arrogance, aggressiveness, and his urge to impress, are all signs of the fragility of his unnatural position in a natural world. When one reads the definition of a schizoid, it is like reading the definition of adolescent male humanity. (. . . "being susceptible to any criticism or situation which threatens the position, assumed attitude of superiority.") Schizophrenia, paranoia, depressions, suicide, or murder do not exist in children. They all start with adolescence, with the development of the mind.

We all agree that men are egotistical, selfish, and aggressive, but these are the characteristics of any psychopath. This is not surprising, however, considering that adolescence is the vulnerable phase of an incomplete and ambitious being. Conceit, self-indulgence, self-centeredness, intolerance, pride, vanity, capriciousness, animosity, spitefulness, revenge, resentfulness, envy, jealousy, hatred, cruelty, agony, ecstasy, and above all self-confidence and self-esteem, are the main characteristics of male humanity in their adolescent phase.

What, we might ask, inspires these characteristics in man?

Belief of superiority is the cause of all these.

Adolescence is an obstinate stage. Occasionally an adolescent reaches the apex of obstinacy, when he believes in miracles.

Adolescents are afraid of the truth. Adolescence is a stage of beliefs, each belief having its own truth. Pascal said: "We make an ideal of truth." In fact man does the opposite; he makes the truth out of an ideal. Without humility man cannot know the truth. The truth is always humiliating for man, which is why he prefers beliefs.

Man lives in an intoxicated state of narcissism until he dies. Any woman will tell you how pathetic man, living among the illusions created by his mind, can be, and how easily he is seduced if these illusions are flattered.

There is nothing more pathetic than an old adolescent faced with reality, a reality which cannot be treated with illusions, the reality of death. When the idea of death enters the head of an old male adolescent, a comedy takes place. Reading the morning papers, he will say to himself: "Life is not worth living any more; the world is going to the dogs." As man is the only animal capable of brainwashing himself, he will convince himself that the "new world" is not for him or his "dignity," thereby fooling himself that death is a blessed relief. He then feels free to make his exit like a great actor performing the role of indignation.

Will the human male ever reach maturity?

Most scientists agree that adolescence is the period of life between biological and social maturity.

What does social maturity mean? What is the meaning of the other maturities that an adolescent likes to flatter himself with, as for instance, legal maturity, political maturity, or moral maturity? What is the meaning of expressions such as sentimental maturity, emotional maturity, academic maturity, or professional maturity? These are all nothing but abstract terms invented by man for specific, abstract reasons, for his needs of the moment. The meaning given to these expressions has changed and will continue to change throughout history, whenever there is a new gang in power.

In my view, a logical definition of adolescence might be the period between biological and mental maturity. Man is a mental animal, and without mental maturity he can not be considered an adult being. As far as the human male's mental maturity is concerned, the history of mankind, dominated by man, is clear evidence that man has not yet achieved it. A being living in a transcendental world can only pose as mature in abstract terms.

Man never advances beyond adolescence because adolescence provides the excitement of extremes. Adolescence is the first mental stage of man in which, as in any first stage, extremes dominate. Extremes give adolescents the impression of living life to the full. Adolescence is either noble or ignoble, but seldom understanding; selfish or charitable, but seldom reasonable; loving or persecuting, but seldom tolerant; cruel or pitying, but seldom indulgent; brilliant or stupid, but seldom wise; good or evil, but seldom fair.

Not only has man never advanced beyond the adolescent phase, but we will now see that whenever he feels that his mind has failed him, he reverts to infancy, a new, a man-made infancy; yet another creation of the human mind.

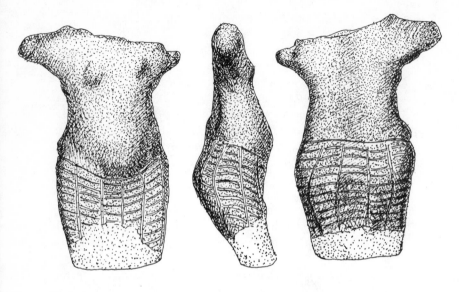

"Figurines of women were no longer naked but clothed."

PART THREE

The Mind in Search of
a Pattern of Life

With the success of the adolescent revolution, the human male took over the human groups. He faced a great problem which is still with us today: the problem of the organization of life. The long-established pattern of life based on the natural mother-infant relationship was broken, and man had to introduce a new one.

But what organization is a being with no instinct or innate pattern of behavior capable of producing?

Faced with this problem, the human male resorted to his mind, that mind which had helped him in his rebellion.

Abstract ideas, prejudices, and ideals were substituted for natural relationships. Later, political, social, religious, and economic ideologies and beliefs took over.

The mind's main difficulty was how to divide the work between the members of the group, the work on which the survival of individuals and collectivity depended. Previously a natural division of labor had existed, based on the mother-infant relationship. With the adolescent revolution, this production-distribution relationship was severed. For the conceited adolescent human male, work was degrading. It was a chore and therefore a punishment. Even today man finds work a sacrifice or a punishment unless it is a hobby or a job in the position of incompetence, which thereby flatters his ego. This self-infatuated adolescent needed a reason to work.

The only way the human male could solve this problem was with his new toy, his mind.

One of man's first abstract thoughts must have been death.

When man realized that he was mortal, he panicked. This sudden realization was the price he had to pay for his mind. He was terrified of his end. Playing with his mind, man tried desperately to overcome this fear. The scar left on the human old brain by the original rebellion gave the human mind the ability to see the other extreme, the antithesis. The idea of death inspired the idea of no death: the idea of eternal life, the idea of immortality.

The human male's pattern of life started by being dictated by immortality. Afterlife governed present life. Man began to organize and even to sacrifice his earthly life to deserve the afterlife invented by his mind.

How did the human brain reconcile eternity with the positive disappearance of life?

The idea of immortality was elaborated by analogy to the regeneration of plants through fallen seeds. The dead human body became the seed, through which new life must appear. The human body or the human head, like the seed, was covered to give growth to a new life.

When humanity realized that nothing grew from a planted corpse, the idea of immortality created the idea of the Underworld. Man convinced himself that there must be another world under the earth where the dead continued to live *ad infinitum*. This idea created the idea of tombs.

Human imagination invented all kinds of Elysian fields, and Hades: heaven for the blessed and hell for the damned. In Virgil's *Aeneid*, Sibyl explained to Aeneas that at one point "where the road splits in twain," in the Underworld, "the right road leads to the giant walls of Dis, our way to Elysium; but the left wreaks doom on sinners, and the guilty Tartarus sends."

Rewards and punishments in the afterlife had to be invented to assist man's idea of heaven and hell. These were connected with the idea of judgment.

Who was the judge?

MAN: THE FALLEN APE

The judge was the god selected by the gang in power, whose criteria of punishment were invented by the gang in accordance with its earthly needs.

How did humanity attain the idea of paradise and of hell?

I have already said that however omnipotent the human mind may be, it cannot create *ex nihilo*. I have also stressed that the mind's creations are programed by the scars left on the human old brain by the experiences of the human species. The idea of paradise must have been inspired by life in the woodlands; the idea of hell by life in the savannah.

The myth of paradise and hell are as old as the human mind's ability to create abstract thoughts. The Sumerians likened Paradise to their ancestors' life in the woodlands, but they saw hell as a sandy, dusty desert, like the savannah.

To Homer, the Elysian plain was "at the end of the world" where "men lead an easier life than anywhere else in the world." Through the mouth of Odysseus' mother, Homer described "the house of Hades and dread Proserpine," as this "abode of darkness" where the damned "perish in the fierceness of consuming fire as soon as life has left the body."

Virgil describes Elysium as "the happy region and green pleasantness of the blest woodlands, the abode of joy," the Tartarus as a place surrounded by "a fierce torrent of billowy fire." The savannah's intense heat, which left a deep scar on the human old brain, has inspired the idea of hell as a permanent fire throughout history. "That hell," wrote St. Augustine, "which is also called a lake of fire, will torment the bodies of the damned."

With the development of intelligence, however, and the realization that bodies putrefied in tombs, human wishful-thinking invented the soul. The soul became immortal. Man's flesh may die, but his soul will live forever.

Herodotus informs us that "The Egyptians were the first to hold the opinion that the soul of man was immortal."

In Plato's *Phaedo*, Socrates explained that when the soul liberates itself from the body it "departs to the invisible world—to the divine and immortal and rational." To Aristotle the soul is "the principle of life in living things." Aquinas stressed that "the human soul which is called the intellect or mind, is something incorporeal and subsistent." To Kant, *summum bonum*, blissfulness, is "only possible practically on the supposition of the immortality of the soul." To Kant, immortality was a moral necessity, it had to exist; it had to exist because human capriciousness imposed it.

Human beings were ready to risk anything to become immortal. Such was the fear, not of the actual death, but that with death there was nothingness. To disappear into nothingness was a terrible outrage, a deep humiliation for self-infatuated human beings. "Leaving behind them a name which shall be eternal," is the supreme aim of man, according to Plato in his *Symposium* . . . "The mortal nature is seeking as far as is possible to be everlasting and immortal. . . ."

When in doubt of an abstract answer about immortality, the mind found that there was only one eventual possible solution: procreation. The one hope left to men was the hope that they would be remembered through their progeny, the hope that the offspring "will preserve their memory and give them the blessedness and immortality which they desire in the future," Plato wrote in the same work. Men "are stirred by the love of an immortality or fame."

In this obsession for immortality we see the reason why man imposed his name on his wife and children. Seneca criticized this human obsession. "The most fatuous thing in the world," he said, "is to marry to have children so that our name is not lost, or so that we have support in our old age, or certain inheritors."

Before he became self-conscious, man's procreation was caused by an obsession with sex. When man became self-conscious, procreation was assured by his obsession of immortality.

Throughout history, the most popular deities have always been those who were resuscitated after death, such as Tammuz, Osiris, Adonis, Attis, Persephone, Balder, and Christ.

In their search for immortality humans invented busts, portraits and self-portraits. It was not the love of art which forced popes, emperors, and kings to order their own portraits; it was one of their ways of remaining with posterity.

Someone rightly pointed out that to scientists, the Nobel Prize or immortality are more important than mankind. I would like to add that this does not only apply to scientists.

Here I quote a passage from an ancient Egyptian text, known

as *In Praise of Learned Scribes.* "Be a scribe, desire that your name may last. A book is more effective than a decorated tombstone. . . . A man is perished, his corpse is dust, all his relatives are dead. It is his writing that makes him remembered in the mouth of the reader."

I also quote two sentences from this century of G. Le Bon from his *Aphorismes du temps présent,* in order to illustrate that the human obsession with immortality is eternal. *"L'homme, confiné par la nature dans l'éphèmere, rêve d'éternité. En élevant des temples et des statues, il se donne illusion de créer des choses qu'on ne verra pas périr."*

The human obsession for giving anything, even life, for immortality, led Freud into committing an error when he stressed that humans possess the instinct of death. Men are indeed ready to risk their life for immortality. But this readiness to die is not caused by instinct, but by the idea of immortality created by the mind.

Man's self-awareness created in his mind the idea of existence. The origin of the word "existence" comes from the Latin *existere.* This is composed of *ex* and *sistere* meaning to cause, to stand, to step forward, to move upward from an inferior to a superior position, i.e.: from mortality to immortality.

I would like to analyze the efforts of man's mind in his search for a new pattern of life by describing the first civilizations. Anywhere in the world, the first pattern of life, after men discovered the mind, was inspired by the idea of immortality, the idea of a life after death.

*

MESOPOTAMIA

The success of advancement of the adolescent revolution varied from peoples to peoples.

Definite evidence of the adolescent revolution can be found among cultural remains in the Balkans, in the so-called Old European Civilization, which flourished in the period between 7000 and 3000 B.C.

Judging by the shrines and figurines found in the Vinča Starčevo and Cucuteni areas belonging to the period of the seventh, sixth, and fifth millennia B.C., religious life was governed by the Great Goddess. This must mean that human groups were still ruled by the mother figure and that society was based on a mother-child relationship.

By the end of the fifth millennium B.C., particularly in the Vinča area, central Serbia and the Sesklo area in northern Greece, figurines of male nudes proudly holding their penises were already in evidence. Another change took place in the same period. Figurines of women were no longer naked but clothed.

In Minoan Crete there was the Mother-Goddess culture and civilization. Women's high position in ancient Crete can be deduced from the artistic remains found in Knossos.

Except for two intermediate periods and for the reign of King Akhenaton, ancient Egypt remained dominated by women, until her end. The two main gods of ancient Egypt, Osiris, god of the underworld, and Horus, the living god, personified in the Pharaoh, owe their positions, the former his immortality, the latter his life, to Isis, the wife of Osiris and the mother of Horus.

There is historical and literary evidence that in China during the Shang dynasty (1766–1123 B.C.) and during the Chou dynasty (1123–256 B.C.), life was influenced by "The Divine Woman" (Shen nü). In China Shamanka (or mother) also had the important role of the oracles which can be seen influencing life even during the T'ang dynasty (A.D. 618–906). "The earliest available evidence shows that in the society of the Chinese bronze age, the Shamanka played a highly important spiritual role," we read in *The Divine Woman* (by E. H. Schafer).

The first historical evidence of a successful adolescent revolution was in Mesopotamia.

"My wife is at the outdoor shrine, my mother is down by the river and here am I dying of hunger." This early Sumerian saying illustrates man's arrogance, and pretentiousness, but at the same time dependence on woman in Mesopotamian society at the dawn of its history. The following Akkadian proverb shows man's successful liberation from woman's domination: "A woman without a husband is like a field without cultivation."

Enuma-Elish, the Sumero-Akkadian epic of creation, explains the victory of the adolescent gang against the domineering

"Enuma-Elish, *the Sumero-Akkadian epic of creation . . .*"

mother. In this epic the young gods chose the god Marduk as their leader to fight Tiamat, the mother of the gods. Tiamat was depicted as a monster dominating the chaos. Marduk kills her, taking from her "tablets of fate," the symbols of power. Then from her dead body he created the universe. Marduk also kills Kingu her husband, "and from his blood creates mankind. . . ."

The adolescent revolution in Mesopotamia changed the basic relationship between man and woman. In the name of his newly discovered strength, man started to force woman, chosen by him, to be faithful only to him. One of the main aims of man's positive legislation, from the first Mesopotamian laws until modern legislation, was to prevent woman from deriding man's self-infatuation and his belief in his superiority, by preventing woman's promiscuity and her economic independence.

In the first known human laws, those of the Sumerian king, Ur-Namu, around the year 2050 B.C., we read: "If the wife of a man, by employing her charms, followed another man, and slept with him, the woman shall be put to death, the man going free."

In the Hammurabi laws of the eighteenth century B.C., unless the husband pardoned his wife caught committing adultery, she was burned.

In Assyrian society women sank to a pathetic and even ridiculous position. "If a woman has crushed a man's testicles in a brawl," says an Assyrian law, "They shall cut off one of her fingers, and if the other testicle has become infected . . . or she has crushed the other testicle in a brawl, they shall gouge out both her eyes." In Assyrian law there was capital punishment for a wife accused of stealing her husband's goods, and his goods even included her own dowry. An Assyrian man was allowed to beat his wife, and even to mutilate her body if he felt so inclined. He was free to divorce her whenever he pleased; the position of her finances were left to him. This situation is illustrated in the following legal rule: "If a man wishes to divorce his wife, if it is his will, he may give her something; if it is not his will he need not give her anything; she shall go forth empty."

Such laws show the vulnerability of man in power. He used his physical, political, economic, and legal strength to impose himself on woman. Man wanted to humiliate woman. He was terrified of being humiliated by her. Man is the only creature in nature who can be humiliated, the only animal who is self-infatuated.

There were two ways in which man could be humiliated by woman. One was her promiscuity, the other her independence. In Hammurabi's code, we read that a man could repudiate his wife without returning her dowry if she "engages in business, thus neglecting her house and humiliating her husband."

Mesopotamian civilization offers a clear picture of the struggle of the human mind in search of a way of organizing life, a struggle which was repeated in other civilizations at other times.

The Sumerian belief in immortality, in life after death, created the idea of tombs where the Mesopotamians buried food, jewels and working tools with their dead. Historical evidence for this was found in the Sumerian tombs of the fourth millennium B.C.

In the third millennium B.C., however, the Sumerian mind started doubting the concept of immortality. In the Sumero-Akkadian *Epic of Gilgamesh*, the King of Uruk, the hero of this popular epic, after a series of vicissitudes, finally obtained the magical plant of eternity from the gods but, alas, a serpent stole it from him, a great disappointment for the Sumerian adolescent mind.

In the following section of this pessimistic epic we can find this message: "For when the gods created man, they let death be his share and life withheld in their own hands."

What then was the purpose of human life? Why did the gods create man?

The epic explains that the gods created man to serve them; to slave for them. Work is for slaves, and therefore it is a punishment. By syllogistic reasoning this belief entertained the belief that whoever had slaves were gods. Serving the gods meant in practical terms slaving for the inventors of gods, who were the gang dominating the temple of the city's god. The chief priest of the temple soon became the king of the city, and judging by the "Sumerian King List" which, although from the beginning of the second millennium B.C. must have reflected the traditions of centuries long past, the powers of kings "descended from heaven."

The exploitation of believers is revealed in the following lines from the Mesopotamian *Dialogues of Pessimism:* "They walk on a lucky path who do not seek a god, those who devoutly pray . . . become poor and weak."

There is little difference between these ancient words on the exploitation of beliefs to the following modern anecdote. A Chinese reproached an American, saying, "In your country man exploits man." When the American asked, "What about your country?" the Chinese answered, "In my country it is the other way around!"

Something else can be deduced from the *Epic of Gilgamesh*. It is revealed that the gods also needed man to work in order to maintain the divine order.

What was this divine order?

It was the opposite of chaos. But what was this chaos so feared by man?

To the adolescent mind, chaos meant a life of promiscuity, a life dominated by women. In the Sumerian creative myth *En-uma-Elish*, the mother goddess, Tiamat (who was killed by Marduk), represented chaos. To the male adolescent the divine order was an order in which he was the center of the universe. That may be the reason why humans took so long to produce a Copernicus.

Increasing doubts about the idea of immorality increased dissatisfaction over the organization of a life based on the belief in an afterlife. This created an atmosphere which is reflected in the text *The Pessimistic Dialogue Between Master and Servant*, particularly in the following passage:

"Servant obey me!"

"Yes, my lord, yes."

"I will do something helpful for my country."

"Do, my lord, do. The man who does something helpful for his country, his deed is placed in the bowl of Marduk."

"No, my servant, I will not do something helpful for my country."

"Do it not, my lord, do it not. Climb the mounds of ancient ruins and walk about: look at the skulls of late and early men: who among them is an evil-doer, who a public benefactor?"

How did the Mesopotamians solve the problem of the failure of their mind?

The human mind found three solutions to solve the problem of gloom and despair caused by its failure to find a solution to the male-organized way of life. These three solutions were Mesopotamia's legacies to mankind: alcoholism, divination, and a pattern of life imposed by codified laws, enforced in the name of an omnipotent and monotheistic God.

The significance of alcoholism (which is derived from a Sumerian word) can be gained by the following verses from a Sumerian hymn:

Drinking beer in blissful mood,
Drinking liquor, feeling exhilarated . . .
The heart of Inanna is happy again,
The heart of the Queen of Heaven is happy again.

In a passage from *Enuma-Elish*, we find how the Sumerian deities used alcohol:

They smacked their tongues and sat down to feast
They ate and drank,
Sweet drink dispelled their fears,
They sang for joy drinking strong wine
Carefree they grew, their hearts elated.

" 'Drinking beer in blissful mood.' "

Here we can understand how the "sweet drink dispelled" even the fears of the mighty gods. For the human mind, alcohol is a necessity. No animal needs alcohol.

The mind's second solution to the problems of life was divination. Astrology was born in Mesopotamia and the reading of animal's lungs, liver, and intestines was born before the invention of writing. The importance of divination in the life of ancient Mesopotamia can be seen in the text *The Lord of Wisdom*.

The third solution to the crisis of the Mesopotamian mind was its main legacy to mankind.

We know that man regressed to infancy when faced with any crisis or despair. Regressing to infancy means going back to *gremio matris*, to the maternal way of life. For the self-infatuated male to go back to his mother, especially in the early stages of his rebellion, would have meant humiliation.

What then could the solution of the Sumerian mind have been, lost in a mental savannah?

The solution was a new invention of the mind, an abstract infancy, a man-made neoteny. The mind invented a father, a strong, omnipotent, and omnipresent father. The Mesopotamian male regressed to an abstract infancy, protected by an abstract father. In that infancy he begged his father to direct him in his life, offering him the only thing a confused mind can offer, obedience. The father, the absolute ruler, the omnipotent god, is the creation of a mind which has failed. An unsuccessful mind is always prepared to obey.

What caused this desire to obey?

It was brought about by a desire for orders, orders which suited the mind. Eagerness to obey orders inspired orders. The human mind's creation "ought to be" inspired human obedience, thus creating authority, power or might in the hands of a god or a ruler, a church or a state. This transformed "ought to be" into "thou shalt." Omnipotent dictatorial gods or rulers were, and will always be, victims of their followers.

Man, who rebelled against his mother in the name of autonomy and freedom, after various exploits of his mind, reverted to obedience, the childlike obedience to a father, an invented might. Man will always be an unself-sufficient and dependent creature.

This example of the Mesopotamians regressing to an abstract

man-made infancy will be repeated throughout history. These periods of infancy will occasionally be broken by adolescent revolutions which, after a spell of the adolescent male-rule of competition, strife, and anarchy, will result in a new phase of abstract infancy with a new god or ruler, a new father figure, a new might. This will be followed by a new adolescent revolution, and so on.

Once an abstract infancy is re-established in a human group, the individuals who do not regress to infancy, those who refuse to conform to it, those who remain in the adolescent phase, will be considered, throughout history, as sinners, heretics, and outlaws. All criminals, revolutionaries, and heretics, of all ages, were, are, and always will be the adolescents in a society of man-made infancy.

It is interesting to note that generally, in these periods of man-made infancy, playing is often forbidden, and games require permission from the authorities. With the advent of Christianity, Emperor Theodosius ended the Olympic Games.

The Mesopotamian people, unable to create a convincing myth about the afterlife through which they could organize their life on earth, created positive laws instead. These laws were inspired and enforced by the earthly authorities in the name of a powerful god.

Codes of law are always created by an absolute ruler or an omnipotent god, in times of confusion of past beliefs, in a moment of capitulation by the adolescent mind, a moment of reversion to paternal infancy.

Judging by the first codified laws which appeared in the middle of the twenty-first century B.C., the laws of Ur-Nammu, and of Hammurabi's laws in eighteenth century B.C., Marduk was clearly the omnipotent, omnipresent and sole god of Babylonia, taking over from Anu and Enlil, the previous great deities of the Mesopotamian Pantheon. He was called Bel, which means the supreme of all supremes. We read this in the seventh tablet of the *Epic of Creation:*

God Enlil: it is Marduk of government;
God Nabu: it is Marduk of opulence;
God Ninurta: it is Marduk of works;

Eighteenth-century B.C. *limestone relief with a figure representing Hammurabi, king of Babylon.*

God Sin: it is Marduk who illuminates night;
God Adad: it is Marduk of rain;
God Nergal: it is Marduk of war;
God Zabala: it is Marduk of battle;
God Shamash: it is Marduk of justice.

In the prologue of Hammurabi's code of laws we read: "Anu and Enlil had endowed Marduk with the supreme power for whom they founded the eternal kingdom in Babylon. . . ."

Why did Marduk become "the strongest of all gods"? The adolescent male, confused in his mind, worshiped strength in his leaders and in his gods. Strength inspired confidence. A confused mind craves confidence.

MAN: THE FALLEN APE

Marduk was better-armed than any other god. In the Sumero-Akkadian *Epic of Creation*, when Marduk, as a leader of a "horde of young gods" goes into battle against the mother goddess, he is armed with a bow and arrow, a streak of lightning . . . a bolt of thunder and seven winds, and riding a chariot of storm drawn by winged dragons breathing fire.

"Your name is the greatest, O ferocious Marduk," we read in a hymn. He is "King of all Gods and of all Kings."

The most important Babylonian festivity, Akitu, shows us Marduk's omnipotence. Akitu was the name given to the New Year celebrations which lasted for twelve days. On the eighth day the king and his dignitaries went to the tower of Babel, in the famous chapel of Marduk, where the "supreme of supreme gods" gave the king of Babylon the orders and predictions for the coming year. Called "The Settling of Destinies," this ceremony was considered the main event of the Akitu festivities. Marduk, the absolute god, reinvested the king of Babylon with absolute power. Religious monotheism and temporal absolutism helped each other throughout the history of male-organized societies. Only a strong god, only a god without competition with other gods, is able to bestow equality on the confused adolescent mind afraid that, through competition, the strong could do better than the weak.

"Mankind, tired out with a life of brute force" . . . "submitted of its own free will to laws and stringent codes." These words of Lucretius, echoed by Rousseau and hundreds of authors and politicians, express a certain truth. They do not explain, however, that the "life of brute force" came with the adolescent revolution, male competitiveness and competition, antagonism, arrogance, and aggression, caused by self-infatuation, the creation of the mind. The human mind, having embraced confusion, its own cul-de-sac, had no alternative but "laws and stringent codes" as the solution to a male pattern of life.

Marduk, in the end, being without competition, was so strong that he was even capable of compassion. In the text of *Lord of Wisdom*, we read that he is the god "whose heart is merciful, whose mind forgiving, whose gentle hand sustains the dying." "The strongest of all gods and all kings," the omnipotent Marduk, "this merciful god," was the terminal outcome of the first adolescent revolution in Mesopotamia.

After centuries of vicissitudes and searching for a pattern of life, the minds of the Mesopotamian people solved their delusions by regressing to infancy, an infancy created by the same mind, an infancy protected by an idealized father, a father created by wishful thinking, the wishful thinking of the masses. The delusions created the masses who were ready to revert to a father-protected infancy.

This idealized father is flattered by the people's worship and obedience. Flatterers will get what they want out of the flattered father. A flattered father is blind, easy to fool, easily led, led by obedience, the instrument by which the masses achieve their aspirations. Obedience is never blind. Obeyed gods and leaders are blind.

The Mesopotamian pattern was repeated throughout history until the time of the modern gods, gods led, used, and abused by the masses, who are only the capricious and spoiled children of a powerful but blind father.

We have seen that in Babylon, Shamash, god of justice was "Marduk of justice." Justice was therefore in the hands of Marduk which he bestowed upon his king on earth each year. We read the following in the introduction of the Hammurabi's code of laws: "I am the king who is pre-eminent among kings: my words are choice, my ability has no equal. By the order of Shamash, the geat judge of heaven and earth, may my justice prevail in the land" . . . "By the word of Marduk, my lord, may my statutes have no one to rescind them!"

What was justice, invented by the human mind?

Before the adolescent revolution there was the mother-infant relationship, based on equity, maternal equity, meaning unequal treatment of unequals. The maternal organization of humanity was based on this principle for more than 16 million years.

With the adolescent revolution man rebelled against this equity. The adolescent revolution introduced adolescent justice, which was expediency, the expediency of the strong. The strong became right. It was in this state of anarchy that human justice, as we know it today, was born. Human justice became another peculiarity of man. Human justice, in essence, is a pleonasm, because justice is always human, it is always created by man's mind. There is no justice in nature, only laws.

The first and the supreme purpose of justice was to prevent the strong from abusing the weak. The first idea of justice, which in essence is in conflict with the primary law of nature, the right of the fittest to survive at the expense of the weak for the sake of the species, must have been inspired by the deep scar left on the human old brain when the humans were expelled from their natural environment by the stronger apes.

The old scar may have been revived by the majority of the weak, by the dramatic experience of the first adolescent revolution.

But who, in the human groups dominated by adolescents, was able to prevent the strong from imposing their strength over the less fit?

The strongest might! It was might, from which the church and the state emerged, that could stop the strong from overrunning the weak. Who represented might in the human groups? The person who commanded the most obedience among the group, whoever could have given the commands inspired by the wishes of the majority and its readiness to obey. The obedience of the majority in a group dictates its justice and imposes it on the strong. The weak, always the majority in any human group, create might. Might and the weak will always be allies against the strong. Might is right because only might can make right, restore broken harmony, do justice, make reparation. Above all, might can vindicate the weak.

In a Mesopotamian document it says that Ur-Nammu, "established justice in the lands and banished malediction, violence and strife." The purpose of Hammurabi's code of laws was "To cause justice to prevail in the land. . . ."

What was the purpose of his justice?

"The purpose of justice is to destroy wicked and evil, that the strong may not oppress the weak. . . ." the text explains.

Abusing the weak was punished in the name of equality, an equality determined by the weak. Equality imposed impartiality on justice.

The aim of man's justice was to prevent injustice, to prevent inequality, to prevent natural laws. Human justice is the invention of a loser or a potential loser. Losers are always the majority. Man's justice is not creative or rewarding in the natural sense; on the contrary.

Man's justice, aiming at preventing injustice and inequality by the punishment of the unjust and of the inequal, uses a simple arithmetical and proportional method, called by the Romans *jus talionis*, a law of retaliation: "an eye for an eye—a tooth for a tooth."

Later, the weak invented so-called "social justice" too. This was inspired mainly by equality in the economic sense, the elimination of visible economic differences. Man knows that social justice in the distribution of wealth seriously prejudices his working productivity, the production of wealth. For man in his abstract infancy, however, economic equality was more important than his economic welfare or his own survival, or that of his progeny or his species.

What was crime?

Crime was anything that broke the harmony and peace created by the tacit or written agreement between the weak and might. In the Sumero-Akkadian *Epic of Creation* the husband of the great mother goddess wanted to destroy the young gods in the name of justice. We read: "Their manners revolt me, day and night without remission we suffer. My will is to destroy them, all of their kind; we shall have peace at last, and we will sleep again."

Aquinas later stated that "Peace is the work of justice indirectly, in so far as justice removes the obstacles to peace. . . ."

A series of crimes considered by the first legislators can be seen in a Sumerian hymn which goes:

Hypocrisy, distortion,
Abuse, malice, unseemliness,
Insolence, enmity, oppression,
Envy, force, libellous speech,
Arrogance . . . breach of contract,
Abuse of legal verdict,

All these evils the land does not tolerate.

All these are characteristics of the adolescent male, and are feared by the weak who have entered an abstract infancy protected by a mighty father—by a church or by a state.

What is punishment? Why should men punish other men?

This subject has interested humanity from Aristotle, Plato, and Protagoras to Kant, Hegel, and Freud, from Aquinas and Dante to Cesare Beccaria, Bentham, Hobbes, Locke, Rousseau, and Montesquieu, and from the Bible to Karl Marx. In the Old Testament punishment was the right to retaliate. To Aquinas, "the order of justice belongs to the order of the Universe and this requires that penalty should be dealt out to sinners." To Hobbes "intemperance is naturally punished with diseases" and "injustice with the violence of enemies." To Kant "Juridical punishment can never merely be administered as a means for promoting another good . . ." "but must in all cases be imposed only because the individual on whom it is inflicted has committed a crime." To Montesquieu, the only reason for punishment was to prevent crime. To Mill, punishment was nothing but "a natural feeling of retaliation or vengeance." In classical Greece punishment was an expediency. In Thucydides we read of Diodotus' protest over the Athenian decision to put the Mitylenians to death. "We are not in a court of justice, but in a political assembly," he stressed, "and the question is not justice but how to make the Mitylenians useful to Athens." According to Freud, humans crave punishment: "The unconscious need for punishment plays a part in every neurotic disease."

Human justice was born from the chaos created during the adolescent revolution. Any adolescent not conforming to the contract between the weak and might was a criminal, a sinner, or a heretic. Only adolescents could be criminals, sinners, or heretics. This implies that no one can be a born criminal, a sinner, or a heretic. It also implies that only man commits crimes, sins, or heresies; a woman seldom does; she does not possess an adolescent mind. A woman can only commit crimes, offenses, or heresies by imitating man, forced by man, or to please man.

What is the purpose of punishment then in a society of abstract infancy?

The purpose of punishment is to correct the criminal or sinner or to convert the heretic. The weak, the masses of any society, the ones who dictate the law of the land, either fear abnormalities or are jealous of them. In either case the weak ask might to eliminate the abnormal, which disturbs the social harmony and above all spoils their peace of mind.

How is this elimination of disturbing abnormalities carried out?

By the physical elimination of criminals, i.e. murder; by getting them out of sight, i.e. expulsion; or by correction.

How are abnormal people corrected or converted?

Abnormal people, such as criminals, sinners, and heretics were, and still are, knocked off their pedestals of adolescent self-infatuation and forced to join the level of the established infancy. This is done by fear, by modern savannahs such as Siberia, but above all by torture and the infliction of physical or moral pain. The aim of this is to humiliate the adolescent, to shake his self-infatuation and his self-confidence.

For man, any physical or moral pain, inflicted as punishment, hurts because it degrades. Man bears great pain without complaint if it is a biological, moral, or aesthetic service. He cries, however, when punished, not so much because it hurts but because it damages his self-infatuation, because it lowers the self-esteem created by his mind. That is why man is more frightened of pain than woman. A woman does not feel degraded by pain: she is seldom in a supernatural state.

In some adolescents, punishment produces pathological consequences, such as regression to very early infancy. This is known as Psychosis Poenalis. The prisoners behave like small infants, often wanting to be spoon-fed, wetting their beds, and even developing stammers and lisps.

As the first purpose of punishment is to correct the criminal or convert the heretic by making him revert to infancy, it is obvious that it would not succeed with a woman. A mother, or a potential mother, could not revert to infancy. Equality of punishment for equal crimes for men and women therefore was, and still is, a great mistake. Punishment for women can only succeed as a deterrent, never as a corrective.

The same punishment for criminals of different ages is also a mistake. Corrective punishment for a child is useless. It cannot make him revert to infancy, he is already there.

There has never been a plausible explanation of *jus talionis*. Why "an eye for an eye" justice?

As I have said, criminals are adolescents—arrogant and aggressive adolescents. How do adolescents externalize their aggression or arrogance? By attitudes or actions that they consider the best way of affirming their superiority.

When the arrogant, aggressive adolescent, by committing a particular crime, found the superiority that he was searching for, the first judge felt that the best way to destroy this superiority, and to demote him to infancy, was by hitting him in the very spot that he had used to achieve his superiority, by hurting him where he had hurt. The first judge knew the true meaning of adolescence. He started his job at the peak of the chaos created by the first adolescent revolution.

The Roman idea of punishing a crime committed with *dolus*, evil intent, more severely than an identical crime committed with *culpa*, negligence, contributes to our explanation of the nature of punishment.

The second purpose of punishment was the prevention of crime—by a deterrent. This is evidence of the sadness of the male organization of life, of the mockery of man's so-called achievements. The only guideline to human behavior that the human male was capable of achieving, was the threat of punishment.

The third purpose of punishment was to give pleasure, orgasmic pleasure to the mediocre, who are only too delighted to watch someone whom they have always been secretly jealous of punished and humiliated.

In cases of excessive adolescent characteristics, punishment fails to succeed as a corrective. These individuals are known as "recidivists" in legal terminology, and "the neurotics" by Freud, who claimed they craved punishment. In my view, the explanation is simpler. Punishment can never succeed as a corrective with individuals with strong adolescent characteristics. Strong adolescents despise the mediocre, their justice and their punishment. This contempt gives them a feeling of superiority and an insensitivity to their pain. Legislators and psychiatrists should look for something else to replace punishment and electric shock treatment, as instruments of correction, in cases of individuals with strong adolescent characteristics. Electric shock is not a treatment, but a punishment. Like any punishment, its purpose is to bring the individual to the savannah, to primordial atavistic fear, to infancy.

Some humans, unhappy in adolescence and in the father-protected infancy, try to find their own way back to the savannah by self-inflicted punishments such as alcohol, drugs, and gambling.

THE INDUS CIVILIZATION

Another instructive consequence of the adolescent revolution can be found in the Indus civilization.

Little is known of what occurred in the Indus Valley until the fifteenth century B.C. What we do know, however, is that between the thirtieth century B.C. and the eighteenth century B.C., there was a highly developed civilization concentrated around the cities of Harappa and Mohenjo-Daro, and that the marvel of this civilization was the drainage system in the cities, and the bathrooms. There is historic evidence that the Indus civilization, at its peak, was dominated by the mother goddess. (And what is more, bathing belonged to female-dominated cultures.) We also know that toward the end of this great civilization, approximately the seventeenth century B.C., there was the cult of the phallus and the bull, indicating male domination and meaning that the adolescent revolution had succeeded. We also know that when the Aryans invaded the Indus Valley from the Northwest, in about 1500 B.C., they met with no opposition. The Harappan culture and civilization had disintegrated; human skeletons lay everywhere, either because there were no survivors to bury the dead, or because there was complete indifference toward death. The once beautiful cities were slums. If one turns back the pages of history, one will discover that great civilizations always disintegrate before being conquered.

What then happened to the Indus civilization?

A little of what probably occurred can be deduced by the artistic remains, such as statuettes and seal impressions, and above all by the legacies of Harappan culture, the main ones being a passive attitude to life, a contempt for work, worship of the god Shiva and the cult of yoga.

In my view, the Harappans reached the peak of their glorious civilization when life was influenced and organized by the Great Goddess. Only in a mother-oriented society could work have been held in such high esteem. Such important technical realizations could only have been achieved where work was honored and revered.

By the seventeenth century B.C. the Harappans were in the adolescent phase. Once in power the Harappan males were lost when faced with the organization of life. In this adolescence they were confronted by a singular absurdity, an absurdity created by a male mind suffering from conceit. When they realized that they were incapable of organizing the daily work necessary for their earthly life, the Harappans became hostile to all earthly activity. Earthly activity brought them face to face with reality and alienated them from their world of conceit. Living became despicable, because work, that essential part of life, was denigrating.

The Harappan adolescent despised life because he was unable to organize it to suit his self-infatuation. It is only a short step from this negative attitude to the glorification of negativism, passivism, and escapism. Soon these negative attitudes became virtues.

The outcome of this negative attitude toward life was starvation, and the result of starvation was yoga. Seal impressions from this period depict yoga positions. Today there are many flattering explanations for yoga, but in reality yoga is nothing but what it was at its origin: the natural adaptation of the body to asceticism, to starvation.

However transcendental the cause of the starvation may be, yoga is just a natural bodily reaction to it. It is somnolence caused by an exhausted and weak body, exhausted by deprivation or starvation. It is a position in which the body uses the least possible amount of its vital energy, a position in which the body can survive longest with the minimum resources.

What was the point of surviving this contemptible life?

The answer can be found in another absurdity of the adolescent mind: exhibitionism. Adolescents enjoy showing off their superiority to life. It was the hallucinatory illusion of superiority created in the brain of a starved body, a starvation brought on by so-called "dignity."

Nirvana, so glorified also by modern escapists, is nothing but a state of mental stupor caused by malnutrition and immobility. The blood of a starved human being starts to concentrate on the vital organs, such as the heart and lungs, at the expense of non-vital organs as the brain. Nirvana is the brain suffused with a minimum flow of blood. Nirvana is not a metaphysical achievement, but a physical phenomenon. It cannot be achieved with a full stomach, however strong the mind or the will.

Anyone who has spent time in a concentration camp can tell you how starvation forces people into all kinds of yoga positions and states of Nirvana. They are simply natural reactions to starvation.

The god Shiva, known as the great "yogi," is another Harappan legacy to mankind. Shiva was a gloomy deity, a fierce deity, a deity of yoga, a deity of lasting death, a deity of the enraged adolescent imprisoned within the cul-de-sac of his mind. That Shiva was a negative and depressing god can be deduced by the necklace made of skulls belonging to his wife, Kali. The necklace was either a present to her from Shiva, or she wore it to please him.

Shiva inspired Buddha's decision, so praised by his followers, to abandon earthly responsibilities, to abandon his wife, his young child, and his species, and to take refuge in a transcendental world, in "contemplation." An animal would never abandon his young and the species in order to "pray" or to "contemplate." Man, the only animal capable of fooling himself, is convinced that he is superior to other animals because he is able to behave unnaturally, to go against the natural law.

The Harappans also became obsessed with copulation, copulation which became more frequent the more difficult life became to organize. The result of this obsession was overpopulation, which contributed to apathy and lethargy.

JEWISH LEGACIES TO MANKIND

The vicissitudes of the Jewish mind in search of a pattern of life has influenced Western history to modern times.

What was the real story of the Jews?

We know that they settled in Egypt during the chaos of the Egyptian Second Intermediate Period, between 1788 B.C. and 1580 B.C., probably having followed the Hyksos, another Semitic people.

The history of the Jews begins with the Exodus.

The Exodus was a great myth, a popular wishful interpretation of some true facts of history. The true facts can be deduced, however, from the mythical explanation.

In order to understand the start of Jewish history better, we must remember that the establishment of the New Kingdom brought a changed atmosphere to Egypt. She became more aggressive and more xenophobic than ever, her nationalism increasing with the foreign occupation. Ahmose, King of Thebes, before he started to liberate Upper Egypt and the Delta, promised a vendetta against even Egyptians who had collaborated with the enemy. The Jews either escaped through fear of the vendetta, leaving everything behind, or were thrown out into the desert by the Egyptians. Whichever the case, the Jews considered this a major humiliation. This humiliation produced a change in the life and religion of the Jews.

I have already stated that a single omnipotent god is the last resort for a humiliated and lost mind. All peoples, when they become too tired to compete, or when they have been beaten, surrender to a paternal and mighty god and his commandments. In other words they revert to a man-made infancy protected by an idealized father.

The Jews, deluded and humiliated, invented Jehovah, inspired, probably, by the Egyptian god Aton. The first commandment issued by Jehovah was: "Thou shalt have no other god but me." This commandment wiped out the entire past from the Jewish mind. Jehovah created a new past, a past which existed even before the Jewish people existed. Jehovah even created things that existed before him. This lack of reason only underlines the uncontrolled rage which the Jewish adolescent mind was experiencing as a result of the expulsion from Egypt.

Jehovah started a dangerous precedent which all new gods and dictators repeated after him: the invention of a new past.

Only the tragedy of expulsion, the humiliation that all Jews shared, could have created national unity under a national god. The Jews accepted Jehovah as the God of Israel.

The fact that the Jews either escaped from Egypt in fear of Egyptian vindictiveness, or were victims of it, can be deduced from Jehovah's main characteristic: vindictiveness against the enemies of Israel. If the story of the Exodus, as told in the Bible, were true, Jehovah would be a happy and generous God, sure of himself and convinced of always being able to outwit the enemy.

That the Exodus was a humiliation, an escape or an expulsion, can be deduced from the popular rage behind the following two verses in Chapter 14 of Exodus: "And the children of Israel went into the midst of the sea upon dry ground: and the waters were a wall unto them on their right hand and on their left" . . . "And the waters returned and covered the chariots and the horsemen, and all the host of Pharaoh that came into the sea after them. There remained not so much as one of them." These two verses are illogical: the illogic of rage. Whoever performed the miracle of parting the waves would never have closed it over the heads of the enemy. A successful performer thrives on admiration, applause, and awe. Any successful god would have closed the sea just before the Egyptians entered it, reveling in their astonishment, applause, and cheers. Nothing satisfies a god more than to convert the enemy into worshipers and admirers.

If the second verse had never been invented, many persecutions of the Jews might have been prevented. Belief in the vindictiveness of a god provokes the persecution of his believers. Belief in the vindictiveness of a god creates arrogance in his believers. The vindictiveness of Jehovah, rooted in the expulsion of the Jews from Egypt, caused a pattern of expulsions throughout Jewish history. This is the sort of paradox that the human mind typically creates. The mind is blind to paradoxes; it loves them; it creates them.

Who is Jehovah?

Jehovah is the god of an exhausted collective mind, a mind which doubts itself. Jehovah is a dictator, a law giver. Jehovah not only gave the law, he gave a written law; and not only a written law but an eternal and immutable law. It was more than a law—it was a series of commandments; yet another evidence of the anger the Jews felt within themselves for their fate. The commandments imply contempt, a low opinion of the commanded. Jehovah gave the Jews no choice or freedom to act. When the Jews had had freedom they had had many gods, but they were unable to unite and were expelled from Egypt.

Commandments were to be obeyed and only Jehovah had the power to enforce them. " 'Vengeance is mine,' said the Lord." The vindictiveness which led the Jews to flee Egypt became God's main weapon in enforcing the commandments.

The Lord's commandments, compared with Mesopotamian laws, were obeyed for fear of vindictiveness, not for fear of justice. Breaking positive laws was a crime punished in proportion to the crime; breaking the commandments was a sin, punished vindictively, and out of proportion. Only fear of this punishment could prevent sin. Unlike crime, sin is a natural inclination. "The fear of the Lord, that is wisdom." This became the motto of all omnipotent gods and dictators. Other gods and dictators, like Our Lord in the Bible, will "take pleasure in them that fear Him."

There is no rational explanation for the commandments. One cannot discuss them or question their true meaning. They do not emanate from speculation, but from revelation. Revelation emerges from the ashes of speculation. Revelation is the hope of a blind mind, blinded by impotence or rage.

The final result of the speculations of the mind concerning the human pattern of life is the "oughts." Revelation imposes commandments. The "oughts" become "thou shalt," or what is even more categorically imperative: "Thou shalt not."

In the Jewish people we find the glorification of obedience, the obedience of an abstract god's law. Here lies evidence that man had no innate pattern of behavior, that he had the instinct neither for preservation of the species nor for self-preservation. Abraham's readiness to sacrifice his son Isaac, in order to obey his god proves this. A Jew will never break the following three commandments, even to save his life: those that deal with worshiping false gods or committing murder or adultery.

The Jews accepted Jehovah's authority and promised to obey his commandments in exchange for Jehovah's promise to treat Israel as a special case and the Jews as the Chosen People.

Between the Jews and Jehovah, as between any other peoples and their gods, there was a pact. The god promised protection in exchange for worship. Every god has his "chosen people"; it is the people who choose him as their only god.

Who invented the revelation?

The prophets. The prophets were representatives of the *vox populi*, the feelings of the masses. The commandments, once given, were there to be kept. Whenever the commandments were broken, a prophet rose to interpret the feelings of the weakest element of the community, pleading with the sinner to return to the way of life of the majority, the mediocre. To the weaker elements, breaking the commandments meant a return to pre-commandment times, times when the stronger ruled the weak.

The prophets were the mouthpiece of Jehovah; "And the Lord said unto me, 'behold, I have put my words in thy mouth.'" Or "Thus spake Jehovah." These were the preludes to the prophecies.

How did the prophets envisage the Lord?

Isaiah's description demonstrates the exalted state of mind in which he saw God. "In the year that King Uzziah died, I saw the Lord sitting upon a throne, high and lifted up, and his train filled the temple. About it stood the Seraphims: each one had six wings; with two he covered his face, and with two he covered his feet, and with two he did fly."

The prophets' public condemnation of sins or sinners was inspired by a fear of returning to the phase of pre-paternal infancy. The accusations were usually against inequality, against those who were more successful, against those who rose above mediocrity.

What infuriated the masses most was that those who sacrificed themselves by keeping the law often ended in misery, and those who disregarded morality, those evildoers who prospered at the expense of naïve peasants, enjoyed a life of luxury. The envy and jealousy of the masses invoked the vindictiveness of God against the wicked, trying to intimidate them into returning to the fold. In the Bible there is much emphasis on intimidation. "The lion hath roared, who will not fear." These are the words of the prophet Amos . . . "It is a fearful thing to fall into the hands of the living God." Isaiah identified the victim of God when he said: "And the mean man boweth down, and the great man humbleth himself: therefore forgive them not. Enter into the rock and hide thee in the dust for fear of the Lord and for the glory of his Majesty." The wicked are hated most. God will turn "upside down the way of the wicked," we read in Psalm 146, and in Psalm 147 "The Lord lifteth up the weak; He casteth the wicked down to the ground."

When the prophets saw that public accusation was not bringing results, they started prophesying doom and catastrophe for Israel, in order to increase the fear of God, revive morality, and organize life more fairly. Predictions of doom were merely intended to increase the fear of God, but it was a terrible surprise when doom and catastrophe actually did strike. With the advent of this tragedy, the prophets were confronted with a real problem. There was nothing left with which to enforce law and the commandments; nothing with which to frighten the sinners. The maximum punishment had already been administered.

After the Assyrian conquest of Israel and the Jewish deportation to Babylon, a significant change took place. The human mind discovered another abstract solution: Messianism. "I will make them one nation in the land, upon the mountains of Israel . . . and David, my servant shall be king over them," thundered the voice of Jehovah, spoken through his prophet Ezekiel.

What inspired the human mind with this concept? The Jews were in a "savannah" leading a life of *provisoire*, waiting to be led back to the woodlands, to the "Kingdom of David."

The "Day of Jehovah," was no longer a day of doom and catastrophe but the beginning of the "Kingdom of God," a realm of glory and eternal happiness. In the "Kingdom of the Lord" men "shall beat their swords into ploughshares, and their spears into pruning-hooks; nation shall not lift up sword against nation, neither shall they learn war any more." When the Messiah creates the "Kingdom of God," Isaiah prophesies: "the wolf shall also dwell with the lamb and the leopard shall lie down with the kid; and the calf and the young lion and the fattling together. And a little child shall lead them. . . ."

What was this "Kingdom of God"?

It was the human mind reverting, once again, to infancy; not an infancy protected by the mother; not an infancy protected by a father: it was a newly invented infancy, it was "life with ancestors." The "Kingdom of God" was an idyllic past, the restoration of a primeval stage, a stage lost over the course of history. The "Kingdom of God" was the ghetto of Eden.

What was this Eden? It was a playground where "the Lord dissolves the commandments," where the forbidden will not exist. "Praised be him who permits the forbidden." This was the motto of Sabbataj Zevi's sect in their sexual orgies on Purim Day.

The aspirations of the Jewish mind in the Babylonian exile was the "Kingdom of Jehovah," an idealized life with their ancestors. What ancestors?

The "Day of Jehovah" was the "Day of Judgment" when all ancestors rose from the dead and the righteous lived forever in the realm of eternal bliss. Previously, the "Day of Judgment" had been the day of the "Visitation of Wrath" upon Israel.

At the beginning of the second century B.C., belief in the coming of the Messiah, as prophesied by Ezekiel, was strong.

Only one question disturbed the mind of the Jews. When would the Messiah come? In order to answer this question the Jews tried to introduce some logic into their minds.

The resurrection from the dead and the "Day of Judgment," had to come after the "Kingdom of Jehovah" was formed, in order to have somewhere to place the righteous ones on the "Day of Judgment." The Messiah, therefore, must come before the "Kingdom of Jehovah" in order to organize it. But, and here is a major "but," the arrival of the Messiah must be preceded by the "End of Days," by the end of earthly kingdoms. What could end the earthly kingdoms? Only a catastrophe, a cataclysm, a general tragedy, a moral and economic chaos. We read in the Bible: "Israel speaks to God: 'When will you redeem us?' He answers: 'When you have sunk to the lowest level, at that time will I redeem you.'"

The idea that the arrival of the Messiah had to come after a catastrophe resulting in the "End of Days" provoked a series of apocalyptic prophecies. Messianism created apocalyptism. Redemption could only be obtained on the ashes of the past and present, on the destruction of the world.

From the idea of messianism came utopianism. It is only a short step from an idealized past to an idealized future.

As messianism and utopianism were the supernatural creations of a frustrated mind they will always remain abstract phenomena —unrealistic and unreal. What possible contact could these abstract phenomena have with reality? They could only become the instigators of apocalyptism, of doom and catastrophe. Messianic or utopian ideas inspire messianic or utopian activism, which is nothing but apocalyptic activism. In more simple terms this means that the main aim of any Utopian is to destroy the world in which he lives. The more one sees of the past and present the more one realizes that messianism and utopianism are nothing but "noble lies," to use Plato's ignoble expression, used when he toyed with his Utopia. People who preach messianism and utopianism in reality want the world in which they live to end, the world in which they are frustrated, frustrated in their ambitions and pretensions. They use messianism and utopianism as an excuse. The danger of "noble lies," unlike ordinary lies, is that they succeed in deceiving and seducing the liar, thus breeding aggression.

Extremists of the West today are well aware that their ideas are rejected even in the countries they worship. They are extremists because they want to destroy the world in which they live their frustrated lives.

Stalin was a great connoisseur of utopians. In order to save the revolution he eliminated all revolutionaries.

The God of Israel promised the Jews redemption when "they had sunk to the lowest level."

What was Jehovah's position, this one omnipotent God, when confronted with the connection between sinking and redeeming?

Jehovah obviously wanted his people in his Kingdom as soon as possible. This implies that he had to help them to reach the "lowest level" as fast as possible. This is an example of the absurdity of the human mind. An omnipotent god helps his people to destroy life merely because he is unable to organize a better pattern of life on the level of self-infatuation.

Now we can ask ourselves if the human mind, reaching the idea of messianism, progressed or achieved anything.

Messianism is nothing but hope, hope being merely a product of desperation, desperation caused by the infatuated mind's pretentiousness. The mind knew this, but being capable of deceiving itself, started glorifying hope. The Christians transformed hope into a virtue. Before the idea of messianism, hope was considered a negative attitude. To Hesiod: "Hope was an evil guide for a needy man." "Far-roving hope, though many have comfort of her," stressed Sophocles, "is to many a delusion that wings the dream of love; and he whom she hounds knows nought till he burns his feet against hot fire." Thus we see hope, yet another fuel for the pretentions of the frustrated.

Women and work occupied a low place in male-dominated cultures.

The Jews entered mythology and history as a male-dominated group. In Chapter 3, verse 16 of Genesis we can realize woman's subordinate position in Jewish society . . . "yet your desire shall be for your husband, and he shall rule over you."

The Jews did not see work as a pleasant or spontaneous activity, even in the Garden of Eden. This comes as no surprise, knowing that the Bible was created by the male mind. "The Lord God took the man and put him in the Garden of Eden to till it and keep it," we read in Chapter 2, verse 15 of Genesis. Man is a servant, employed by God, who ·is a giver of commandments. (Work was demanded.)

After God expelled Adam and Eve from the Garden of Eden, work became His punishment to mankind. In Chapter 3, verse 17, 18, and 19 of Genesis we read: "And to Adam he said, Because you have listened to the voice of your wife, and have eaten of the tree of which I commanded you, You shall not eat of it, cursed is the ground because of you; in toil you shall eat of it all the days of your life; thorns and thistles it shall bring forth to you; and you shall eat the plants of the field. In the sweat of your

MAN: THE FALLEN APE

face you shall eat bread till you return to the ground, for out of it you were taken; you are dust, and to dust you shall return."

How did God execute this punishment?

"Six days you shall labor. . . ." It was a commandment.

GREECE

Ancient Greece offers us the clearest picture of the adolescent revolution. The history of ancient Greece is also important, because no other country, either before or since, has dedicated such mental energy to finding a pattern of life.

When the ancient Greeks entered mythology and history they were in their pre-adolescent phase. Male humanity in this phase is best described in the *Iliad* and the *Odyssey*. It is a phase in which male humanity and the male deities play and explore exuberantly in open spaces returning, however, sooner or later to their women.

Homer's characters invoke the mother's help with every problem they face. When Achilles realized that Agamemnon had taken Briseis, his slave girl, he cried: " 'Mother, you bore me doomed to live but for a little season: . . . Agamemnon, son of Atreus, has done me dishonour, and has robbed me of my prize by force.' He wept aloud as he spoke . . . and his mother heard him and said: 'My son, why are you weeping? What is it that grieves you? Keep it not from me but tell me, that we may know it together.' " This was the behavior of Achilles, the strongest of all men.

The dialogue between Achilles and Hector illustrates the boyish mentality of Homer's heroes.

"Come nearer so that sooner you may reach your appointed destruction." To these words of Achilles, Hector answers: "Son of Peleus, never hope by words to frighten me. As if I were a baby. I myself understand well enough how to speak in vituperation and how to make insults."

Play was the essence of the entire Trojan War. At one point, while keeping Helen, Paris proposed to return all the stolen treasures, adding even some of his own, to end the war. The Greeks rejected the offer. The war was a case of bad humor over a toy, a

"The dialogue between Achilles and Hector illustrates the boyish mentality of Homer's heroes."

bad humor which prolonged the show and the adventures. Helen was the toy. Paris risked the life of Troy and the Trojans for her. We must not forget that at this stage love did not exist.

In the world of Homer, nothing was tragic, not even death. Death merely caused a temporary sorrow, sorrow for having lost a playmate. Even the horses of Achilles were said to lose their playmate. This sorrow soon passed; there were no attachments in the stage of pre-adolescence. Transcendentality was, as yet un-derdeveloped.

The gods of Homer's pantheon were anthropomorphic gods, humans' playmates. In the Trojan War the gods too played at war, some helping one side, some another. They even played tricks on humans. Agamemnon complained that he was a victim of one of these tricks, when he took Achilles' mistress, Briseis, the slave girl. "Not I was the cause of this act," he claimed, "but Zeus, and my portion and the Erinyes who walks in darkness: They, it was, who in the assembly put wild *ate* (temptation) in

MAN: THE FALLEN APE

my understanding, on that day when I arbitrarily took Achilles' prize from him." Like a child, he adds: "So what could I do? A deity will always have its own way." Agamemnon was sorry. He wanted to do anything to repair his error. "But since I was blinded by *ate* and Zeus took away my understanding, I am willing to make my peace and give abundant compensation," he said. Ate was a temptation, an example of bad humor, an impulsive action characteristic of pre-adolescence. In this case, Achilles' slave girl was merely the toy.

When these playful children in the *Iliad* force the play too far, and out of control, they blame *menos*, a diabolical spirit which is placed in their breast by some deity. Penelope, speaking of Helen, said: "Heaven put in her heart to do wrong, and she gave no thought to that wrong-doing, which has been the source of all our sorrows."

Zeus was even cross with humans because they accused the gods of their own errors. In the *Odyssey* he says that "men complain that their troubles come from us; whereas it is they who by their own wicked acts incur more trouble than they need." This sounds a little like children accusing each other over a broken window.

"*The gods of Homer's pantheon were anthropomorphic gods, humans' playmates.*"

In the world of Homer, the dominating characters were the women. While male humanity and the gods played at war, Demeter, the goddess of agriculture worked in the fields. While Odysseus enjoyed adventures around the world, Penelope was working and running the household responsibly and patiently. In the thick of the chaos of the Trojan War, Andromache addressed Hector: "Dear husband, your valour will bring you to destruction; think on your infant son, and on my hapless self who ere long shall be your widow."

This early adolescence of Homer's male world, is best illustrated in Odysseus' adventure on the island of Ogygia. Calypso promised Odysseus that if he remained with her he would gain immortality. He refused this precious gift, preferring to go home in the end. He wanted to go back to Penelope. It is in the nature of a pre-adolescent to return home in the end. He is not an individual yet, but the member of a group, a female-dominated group. In order to become an individual an adolescent must cut his umbilical cord at the doors of his *oikos*, his household. The human male cannot become fully adolescent without killing his mother or destroying her domination. Oikos, this large household governed by women, in Homer's world, had to be destroyed in order for the male to attain full adolescence, replacing it with his father-dominated family. *Agathos* characteristics in Homer's times were nobility, solidity, patience, and hard work—the main characteristics of women.

To sum up the relationship between woman and man in the world of Homer, I quote from the penultimate verse of the *Odyssey:* "Thus spoke Athena, and Odysseus obeyed her gladly."

Other writers agree that the world of Homer was a world of shame-culture. Shame can only be inspired in male humanity by the mother or by the maternal organization of oikos.

The *Iliad* and the *Odyssey* are epics of space. The Homeric world was a wide-open world. Humanity influenced by women is cosmopolitan in its character.

When man discovered the power of the mind, he discovered agoraphobia. Agoraphobia must have inspired the idea of *polis*. Polis confined space. Sumerians, reaching their full adolescence, built their city-states. The Egyptians, who never achieved full adolescence, were more of a nation-state than a city-state.

My thesis that the higher a woman's position in society, the more honored is work, is confirmed by Homer's Greece. The *Iliad* and the *Odyssey* are filled with descriptions of both the gods and the people working. Work is described in minute detail, which would never have happened had it been a boring or humiliating activity. We read of Apollo building the wall of Troy; Hera, the wife of Zeus, dealing with his chariot and his mules herself and Paris happily building his own house. Odysseus talks proudly about his nuptial bed: "which I made with my very own hands" . . . "I built my room around this with strong walls of stone and a roof to cover them and I made the doors strong and well-fitting," he adds. Odysseus says to his father: "I see, sir, that you are an excellent gardener" . . . "I trust, however, that you will not be offended if I say that you take better care of your garden than of yourself."

I have stressed that Homer's society was a co-operative society. How did this co-operation work? What were the rules for the division of labor?

The answer to this can be gathered from a verse in the *Odyssey:* "My delight was in ships, fighting, javelins and arrows," explains Odysseus. "Things that most men shudder to think of; but one man likes one thing and another another, and this was what I was most naturally inclined to."

The division of labor must therefore have followed the principle of "most natural inclination." This was the basis of co-operation and economic productivity in the world of Homer.

The Transitional Period

At about the beginning of the ninth century B.C., the Homeric world ceased to exist, opening the door to the Archaic period. This tumultuous period of Greek history was the transition of Greek male humanity from early adolescence to full adolescence.

With adolescence, the male in Greece faced the problem of the organization of life. The pattern of life in Greece, as with other adolescent revolutions, became the will of the leader of the gang. The gangs started separating from the mother-dominated communities, forming their typically adolescent creation, the polis, the city-state. The leader of each polis became the absolute ruler of the men and women whom he had succeeded to seduce, or force to follow him.

At the start of its formation, the polis must have been a small unit. By the end of the sixth century B.C., there were more than six hundred city-states in Greece, some of them still very small.

The leader of the gang became the king of the city-states, dividing the land of the new city-state between the most combative members of his gang. This was a major transition from the collective possession of land on which the female organization of the human groups was based, to the private ownership of land on which the male organization of the human groups started to be based. The collective possession of the female-dominated group was the land cultivated by the group. Private property was an invention of man's mind. Man transformed a temporary possession of land into a permanent one, by indicating his intention of keeping it, even if by his negligence it lay waste, and even if it gave the impression of being *res nullius*. (Later, Roman legislators called this desire to keep land in sole possession *animus*. This individual animus, added to *corpus*, transformed private possession into private property.) From the beginning of his adolescent revolution, man knew that his independence and his superiority needed something positive to lean on. He knew that innately he had nothing to make him either independent or superior. Private property is a creation of the adolescent male, a creation of his antagonism and competitiveness. The reason for "mine" was to oppose "thine." Land became inalienable, thus transforming the descendants of the members of the gang into the ruling class, the aristocracy. This aristocracy governed the city-states until the end of the seventh century B.C., until the appearance of the plutocrats, the people with money, money that could buy power by indebting the landowners or their heirs.

What was woman's position in this gang-type civilization?

In the world of Homer, man respected woman. The human male, in order to become an adolescent, has to free himself from his respect. The only way to free himself from his respect is to fight respectability and those inspiring it. Fight meant victory and victory meant enslaving the enemy. Woman became the slave of man. In that position he was less afraid of her mocking his conceit.

From a position of respect woman became the object of contempt. Even mythology changed. When Prometheus illegally gave man fire, Zeus, in order to compensate this advantage, gave man a "plague" to live with: "Damnable race of women." Furies or destructive natural forces became female. (Even today hurricanes are given female names.)

In his *The Theogony*, Hesiod relates a popular tale which marked the changing times. Metis, the goddess of Wisdom, was pregnant. Zeus, fearing that her unborn child would be greater than he, thereby becoming his substitute, swallowed her. She was the last deity of wisdom in the Greek Pantheon.

In the seventh century B.C., Semonides of Amorgos introduced malevolence, which became a Greek characteristic, in denigrating women. Semonides claimed that Zeus created the female brain from the brains of all sorts of animals.

The feminine characters that the Greek male mind invented, from Alcestis and Antigone to Clytemnestra, Medea and Phaedra, show, however, that Greek men never really liberated themselves from their fear of women.

This latent fear forced the ancient Greeks to extremes of adolescence, extremes never before or after achieved by anyone. In these extremes we see the reasons for Greek competitiveness, antagonism, egocentrism, disunity, philosophy, narcissism, and homosexuality.

What had happened to Homer's playful gods?

Adolescence is an age of tragic seriousness and purposefulness, an age which abhors play. Zeus, no longer a joyous, playful god, became the powerful father of the pantheon, inspiring the domineering father of Greek families.

Because of their extreme characteristics of adolescence, the Greeks even started fearing each other. They began to be victims of each other's competitiveness, antagonism, boasting and *hubris*. A poor or weak man was merely a victim of the stronger or more aggressive man, and it was inadvisable for the poor man to react. In the *Works and Days* of Hesiod, written in about 700 B.C., we read: . . . "for hubris is harmful to a poor man." This defenselessness against the stronger is illustrated in the same works of Hesiod by the following fairy tale, where the hawk is talking to his victim the nightingale: "Miserable creature, why do you lament? One who is far stronger than you has you in his grip, and you shall go wherever I take you, singer though you be; and I shall either make you my dinner or let you go as I choose. He is foolish who tries to resist the stronger, for he is bereft of victory and suffers woes in addition to disgrace."

What could the solution be for the victims of hubris?

Justice! Zeus became justice! He had to protect the weak and poor. Hesiod expressed the feeling of the masses when he stressed: "But for those who practice *hubris* and harsh deeds, Zeus . . . doles out a punishment. Often even a whole city suffers because of one man's wrong, and his presumptiveness."

In the human jungle, in which the stronger survived, Hesiod produced another wish of the masses: "For Zeus has established this law for men, that fishes, wild beasts and winged birds should eat one another, for they have not justice among them; to mankind, though, he gave justice, which proves to be much the most beneficial."

Success and fame became an obsession in any field and at any price, success, and fame in economy being the most important. Wealth, giving the best sense of security, became the supreme aim. Money—economy, which started then, helped unscrupulous adolescents in their aspirations. Money created debts, and debts created slaves and servants. This meant wealth and power. This can be deduced from the writings of Theognis of Megara who said: . . . "for the majority of people there is only one value—wealth."

The masses soon realized, however, that the justice of Zeus did not succeed. Hubris was producing success, fame, wealth, and the good life, at the expense of the weak. The masses found another consolation. Zeus may not punish the arrogant but he will punish their progeny.

Soon, however, some were not happy that god should punish the innocent progeny for their unjust ancestors. Theognis registered this feeling by saying: "that the wrongful deeds of the father should not bring harm to his children, and that the children of an unjust father, who were themselves just . . . should not pay for the transgression of their father. . . . As it is, the man who does wrong escapes, and another man pays for it after."

By the year 620 B.C., general confusion produced a dramatic

reaction. The people began to accept the toughest human justice that had ever been, the justice of Draco. Most offenses received the death penalty. Plutarch rightly claimed that Draco "wrote his laws in blood."

The start of the sixth century B.C. brought Solon, a much wiser Athenian legislator. The aim of Solon's laws was to restrain "obsession for wealth," "restrain excess," and "establish order." What class of order? Solon answers "the old order." To understand the quest for "the old order" I must explain another phenomenon of adolescence.

Adolescence produces a permanent war between two generations, fathers and sons. The hubris of the new generation, their "obsession for wealth," could only go against the wealth of their fathers. Solon wanted the new generation to exercise moderation, to show respect for their fathers. His first aim was made clear in these lines from one of his poems: "I desire to possess wealth, but not to possess it unjustly; just punishment always comes afterwards; the wealth that the gods give remains with a man permanently . . . whereas the wealth that men pursue by hubris does not come in an orderly decent manner, but against its will, pursued by unjust deeds; and swiftly disaster is mingled with it. . . ."

Solon tried to reinforce this respect by changing the law of succession. He gave the father more freedom in making his will, even permitting him to emancipate his slaves; this was also done to make slaves more obedient and respectful.

With this move toward more respect for fathers, the story of Oedipus passed through a metamorphosis. Intended as an amusing misunderstanding, Oedipus was transformed into a tragedy dramatized by Sophocles. In the old version, Oedipus remained the King of Thebes until his glorious death and ceremonial burial.

Solon knew that divine justice could only work if it was helped by human justice. Only by helping Zeus with his positive laws could Solon claim, in his famous Eulogy, that Zeus, in spite of everything, was a just and fair god.

According to Plutarch, who wrote his life story, Solon, having seen the negative consequences of provisional times, fixed the duration of his laws for one hundred years. His aim was to reach a state of *eunomia*, a word interpreted as the "good laws," "good order," "just distribution," or the "obedience to laws." In my view, his aim was stability. He must have known that the main cause of hubris was instability.

In order to please or appease the Greek male adolescents, Solon expressed his contempt for woman in his legislation. Woman's influence was considered dangerous, therefore her juridical position was reduced even more, limiting her rights of property.

Woman's position declined continuously. Hesiod called her Kalon Kakon—a beautiful catastrophe. (Judging by *Zorba the Greek*, times in Greece have not changed.)

If my thesis that the higher the woman's position in society the more honored the work is true, work in Greece from the time of Homer must have deteriorated considerably. And in fact this was so. By the sixth century B.C., work was for slaves and servants.

In Hesiod's age work meant "inevitable evil." It was called *ponos*. Some writers explain that from this word the Latin word *poena* emerged, meaning suffering.

The Archaic Age in Greek history ended with a desperate plea by the Greek Gnomic poets and didactic popular sayings, for *sophrosyne*.

Sophrosyne is one of those untranslatable Greek words which means "be reasonable" and "keep your intelligence clear of your mind, as the mind is the source of hubris." The following advice from Sophocles in *Antigone* explains the real meaning of sophrosyne. "For old anonymous wisdom has left us a saying: 'of a mind that god leads to destruction, the sign is this—that in the end its good is evil.' Not long shall that mind evade destruction."

With the increased confusion of the second half of the sixth century B.C., the Greek mind opened a new path in the search for a pattern of life. Philosophy was born. The mind, through its abstract speculation, started groping for the truth, the basic, natural or cosmic truth on which to build a pattern of life. Greek adolescents, encouraged by this new infatuation, persuaded themselves that the human mind was able, through speculation, to find a rational explanation of life and therefore to close the dark chapter of mythology.

In their self-confidence and beginners' enthusiasm, the first philosophers took an extreme anti-mythological attitude. In Xenophanes of Colophon, we read the following: "Homer and Hesiod have ascribed to the gods all things that are a shame and a disgrace among men, thefts and adulteries, and the deception of each other." According to Heraclitus, "Homer should be turned out of the lists and whipped, and Archilochus likewise."

Philosophy did, however, make one major contribution to humanity. In its search for the primeval, philosophy opened the way to science. But this contribution could not compensate for the damage it has created throughout history, for philosophy always stoops sooner or later to some belief, and therefore to aggression.

One of the first philosophers was Pythagoras. His speculations may have helped him to discover important mathematical laws, but as far as the general principle of life was concerned, his philosophy resulted in belief, a belief of the transmigration of souls. A similar belief, known as Orphism existed already in Greece, but Pythagoras' scientific spirit was not happy with the passive attitude toward life encouraged by Orphism. He created a religious order, which by practical deeds taught the best way of life. The rule that the novices of this order remained in total silence for five years, gives us an indication that Pythagoras had discovered that men were wasting a great deal of energy by speculation and discussion.

In fact, mental activity consumes much energy, leaving less for physical and practical needs. It has been proved that a man of the same age, weight, and height as a woman consumes for the same amount of work more calories per hour than the woman. In my view, this is because of the extra energy consumed by man's active mind while working. Children, whose minds are undeveloped, have far more energy, than adults. We find many periods in history where, with the increased mental activity of a people, there is a decrease in their collective productivity. The collapse of great empires is always preceded by an increased restlessness of mind among the people who built that empire.

Man's energy, in contrast to that of other animals and that of the human female, does not follow a pattern of innate preferences or priorities, because man has neither an innate pattern of behavior nor an innate scale of priorities. Sublimation, the pillar of psychoanalysis which should be an "unconscious process by which a sexual impulse, or its energy, is deflected, to express itself in some non-sexual, and socially acceptable, activity," as we read in *A Dictionary of Psychology* by J. Drever, is a fallacy. Man's energy is free energy, which is spent pursuing his own personal wishes of the moment, dictated by his mind. Any time the mind decides to concentrate on itself, it consumes so much energy that it leaves very little for other activities. In extreme cases of exaggerated mental activity, as happens with schizophrenics or philosophers, there is no energy left for the elementary needs of the body, or for the social and economic life. When drugs or electric shocks reduce the mental activity of people, thereby reducing the consumption of their energy, they put on weight.

One of the first rational and practical men in history, Confucius, considered it superfluous and derogatory to deal with transcendentality. In fact, his "ideal of normality" transformed the Chinese into the most practical and efficient people in the world.

The Fifth Century B.C.

With its achievements in art, literature, politics, and philosophy, the fifth century B.C. in Greece is considered one of the greatest centuries in the history of mankind.

Ancient Greece, and particularly its fifth century B.C., like childhood for Freudians, resembles a public library where all select what they want to read. From fanatics of democracy to fanatics of fascism, from admirers of art to worshipers of money, from runners in the Olympic Games to runners-away from battlefields, from lovers of competition to partisans of the physical elimination of political opponents, and from hypocrites to homosexuals, they all find facts to suit or justify their preconceived ideas, their pre-assumed attitudes or their actual deeds.

Why was ancient Greece, and particularly its fifth century so glorified and is this glorification justified?

The poetic view of ancient Greece is due to the fact that she was discovered for the first time by the Renaissance and glorified for political reasons, and for the second time by the British and French romantics and the German idealists of the nineteenth century.

"All kinds of competition, from drama to athletics . . ."

In my view, the Golden Century was in fact, one of the most tragic periods of Greek history, which has left damaging legacies to the world. In this period, the human mind entertained not only dangerous absurdities but also the conceit of being proud of them.

Never in the history of mankind has man reached such extremes of adolescence and freedom of mind as in the fifth century B.C. in Greece. The mind became so infatuated with itself that every Greek considered himself the center of the universe, each man having his own personal cult or belief in which he felt the greatest. All kinds of competition, from drama to athletics, from riding to riddle guessing, were invented, the aim being that everyone excelled in something. Each man created a new game to suit his own personal abilities. In my view, it was not the Greek sporting spirit which inspired these games, but the desire to excel. Games were not a sport in Greece, they were a means to an end. Competition was *agon*, antagonism—agony. The competitor was an adversary, a dangerous opponent to be either humiliated or eliminated, by any means. Adolescence is a belligerent stage.

The Greek male found that his mind was omnipotent. Oratory became the means of convincing itself of its own omnipotence. Out of this game came Sophism.

Sophism became so popular that leaders had to open schools all over Greece to teach this new philosophy of life to the self-infatuated Greeks.

What was Sophism, this Greek legacy to mankind?

Protagoras, the leader of Sophism, established the principle of his philosophy by stressing that "man is the measure of everything." This suited the Greek male. Everything became a matter of expediency.

Plato described a Sophist as "the practicer of an art of deception who, without real knowledge of what is good, can give himself the appearance of the knowledge."

To Aristotle, a Sophist was "an impostor who pretends to knowledge employing what he knows to be false for the purpose of deceit and monetary gain. . . ." Aristotle should have added political power. It was, in fact, in the political field that Sophism became so destructive in Greece and subsequently damaging to the world. Sophist demagogy, with its hypocrisy and corruption, produced democracy. This was the discovery of the human mind in the fifth century B.C. in Greece and was another Greek legacy to the world.

Greek society, where wealth and money were signs of superiority soon transformed the fit and unfit into the rich and the poor, the oligarchs and the demos. This produced two contrasting ideas, and divided the Greek world into two opposing sides. One side was obsessed with the production of wealth, the other with social justice and the distribution of wealth, both sides accusing each other of inhumanity and exploitation. The oligarchs claimed that the demos wanted to build a political and economical system, in which the unfit would survive at the expense of the fit, a system which would be "calculated to give an undeserved ascendancy to the poor and the bad over the rich and the good," as one reads in a political leaflet of the fifth century B.C. The demos accused the oligarchs of using their economic power and their political institutions to exploit the poor.

"Betrayal and treason were national pastimes for the Greeks" writes R. Littman in his *The Greek Experiment*. "The Peloponnesian War began with a betrayal," he explains. "During the course of the war there were at least twenty-seven betrayals or attempted betrayals of the cities."

The corruption, dishonesty, and betrayal embraced by the Greek mind in this period remained a part of Greece for a long time. Polybius, some two and a half centuries later, wrote: "Those who handle public funds among the Greeks, even though the sum may be merely a talent, take ten account-checkers, and ten seals and twice as many witnesses, yet they cannot be faithful to their trust. . . ." "Graeculus" (an expression of contempt that the Romans used for the Greeks) was feared by the Romans—judging by Virgil's sentence *"Timeo Danaos et dona ferentes"* —even when bringing gifts.

Demagogy, hypocrisy, and democracy are best illustrated through the attitude and deeds of Pericles, who dominated a third of the fifth century B.C. in Greece.

Here I quote his famous speech delivered in memory of the fallen fighter in the battle of 431 B.C. This speech, recorded by

Thucydides became a bible for the Democrats, the leaders of the masses, the leaders of the "popular" parties.

Our form of government does not enter into rivalry with the institutions of others. We do not copy our neighbours, but are an example to them. It is true that we are called a democracy, for the administration is in the hands of the many and not of the few. But while the law secures equal justice to all alike in their private disputes, the claim of excellence is also recognised; and when a citizen is in any way distinguished, he is preferred to the public service, not as a matter of privilege, but as the reward of merit. Neither is poverty a bar, but a man may benefit his country whatever be the obscurity of his condition. There is no exclusiveness in our public life. . . . While we are unconstrained in our private intercourse, a spirit of reverence pervades our public acts; we are prevented from doing wrong by respect for authority and for the laws, having an especial regard for those which are ordained for the protection of the injured, as well as those unwritten laws which bring upon the transgressor of them the reprobation of the general sentiment. . . . We are lovers of the beautiful, yet simple in our tastes and we cultivate the mind without loss of manliness. Wealth we employ, not for talk and ostentation, but when there is a real use for it. To avow poverty with us is no disgrace; the true disgrace is in doing nothing to avoid it. An Athenian citizen does not neglect the state because he takes care of his own household; and even those of us who are engaged in business have a very fair idea of politics. We alone regard a man who takes no interest in public affairs, not as a harmless, but as a useless character; and if few of us are originators, we are all sound judges of policy. The great impediment to action is, not discussion, but the want of that knowledge which is gained by discussion preparatory to action. For we have a peculiar power of thinking before we act, and of acting too, whereas other men are courageous from ignorance but hesitate upon reflection. . . . To sum up, I say that Athens is the school of Hellas, and that the individual Athenian in his own person seems to have the power of adapting himself to the

MAN: THE FALLEN APE

most varied forms of action with the utmost versatility and grace. This is no passing and idle word but truth and fact; and the assertion is verified by the position to which these qualities have raised the state. . . . For we have compelled every land and every sea to open a path for our valour, and have everywhere planted eternal memorials of our friendship and of our enmity. Such is the city for which these men nobly fought and died; they could not bear the thought that she might be taken from them; and everyone of us who survives should gladly toil on her behalf.

Now I will analyze the objective reality which existed in Athens and which was known to Pericles when he uttered this famous sample of demagogy.

When Pericles glorified democracy he knew that he was the absolute ruler of Athens, who had obtained power by bribing the demos, the masses, and who had expelled all political opponents from Athens. Pericles knew, too, that he was the main architect of the most atrocious war of the ancient world, a war which lasted for twenty-seven years. He depended upon the support of the demos, and he purposely kept the war going to distract attention from their miserable conditions. In the Athens of Pericles, the cradle of so-called democracy, equality, and freedom, out of the 350,000 inhabitants there were only 35,000 rightful citizens. Women, slaves, and foreigners were the object but not the subject of the law. In 451 B.C., Pericles restricted the right of the citizenship of Athens even further.

Under Pericles, woman's position sank to its lowest depths. Even in Sparta, so badly depicted by worshipers of Greek democracy, the judicial, social, and economic position of woman was higher. "The greatest glory of woman," explained Pericles, "is that her name whether for good or ill, should be as little as possible on the lips of man." This was the moral teaching of a man who left his family and lived publicly with Aspasia, a *hetaira*. This contempt for women was yet another legacy of the Periclean age, to the Greeks and to the world. Demosthenes, another great Athenian democrat and demagogue, said: "We have wives for child-bearing, *hetairae* for companionship, and slaves for lust."

Aristotle considered woman even more inferior than did Plato, mainly because of her poor abilities for abstract thinking. Given this low opinion of woman, her conquest was not considered an achievement. The conquest of a male, however, particularly a young boy, was considered a success. Adultery in Greece was not a sentimental or moral offense, but a property offense.

In Pericles' Athens, foreigners were the barbarians, only tolerated if they were useful to the Greeks. Previously "barbarians" referred to those who spoke a foreign tongue. Aristotle repeated the view of Euripides on the inferiority of foreigners when he said: "It is right and reasonable that Greeks should rule over barbarians, for the latter are slaves by nature and the former are free men."

Slaves were treated abominably, most of them working in appalling conditions in the state-owned mines of Laurion and Maroneia. In Aeschylus' *Prometheus* we read the following advice: "Slave, obey your masters in matters just and unjust."

An example of how the Athenians obtained their slaves is shown when they crushed the rebellious Scione, killed all the male population, and enslaved the women and children.

Justice in the Athens of Pericles, so glorified by many writers, was often nothing but an entertainment for the demos. The law courts were in public places, and the jury, selected from loafers or those wandering around the marketplace waiting to be paid or bribed, was composed of at least 500 members. (The jury which condemned Socrates consisted of 501 members, of which 281 found him guilty, therefore to die, and 220 not guilty.)

It was not democratic justice, it was a demos' justice. No woman, slave, or foreigner stood a chance against this kind of jury. A learned or rich man lost his case if he addressed the jury in his own language and in his own cloth. (Any Mediterranean group of poor people or loafers, even today, take pleasure in deriding those who differ in some way from themselves.)

From Lysias' twenty-fifth speech, we see what pleased the jurors, when reading the plea of a defendant: "I made many contributions of money to public finances; and I performed the other 'liturgies' in a manner not inferior to any other citizen. And I spent more money on these than I was required to do by the city, so that I might be thought more *agathos* by you, and if some misfortune should come upon me, I might be judged with more sympathy by the court." In Lysias' third speech we read the address of another defendant to the Athens jury: ". . . and do not overlook the fact that I am being unjustly expelled from my country, for which I have endured many dangers and performed many liturgies and have never caused it any harm, neither I nor any of my relatives, but rather many good deeds." From these speeches we see that spending money on liturgies, enabling the lazy and poor of the city to enjoy life or find something to do, was an important, sometimes even decisive, circumstance on which the verdict of the jury was based.

Athenian international inter-cities justice was pure expediency. This expediency is evident in Thucydides' description of an Athenian representative addressing the following words to the representatives of the small city-states of Melos, defeated by the Athenians: "You know as well as we do that right, as the word goes, is only a question between equals in power, whereas the stronger do whatever they must." The same writer describes Cleon's advice to the Athenians on how to deal with the rebellious Mytilenians in the following lines: "You will do what is just towards the Mytilenians and at the same time what is expedient. . . . For if they were right in rebelling, then you must be wrong in ruling. . . ." Whether the Mytilenians were right or wrong, Cleon concludes his speech with the words "You must punish the Mytilenians as your interest requires."

In *The Republic*, Thrasymachus expressed the general opinion on justice and international justice when he said: "I proclaim that justice is nothing but the interest of the strong. . . ."

Another of Pericles' legacies to the world was ostracism. Ostracism was the banishment of political opponents from the country.

In *The Greeks and the Irrational*, E. R. Dodds explains this: "But the evidence we have is more than enough to prove that the Great Age of Greek Enlightenment was also, like our own time, an Age of Persecution—banishment of scholars, blinkering of thought, and even (if we can believe the tradition about Protagoras) burning of books." In fact, Plato wanted to burn the works of Democritus. This wish, like many of Plato's wishes, was fulfilled in the end by Christianity.

What was the reason for the persecution of political opponents?

Political and religious persecutions were and still are carried out by demagogues playing with the ignorant masses. Demagogues only succeed during an era of corruption and bad faith. They succeed by accusing their opponents of corruption or impiety. This arouses the false indignation of the masses. Nothing is more aggressive than the false indignation of the masses. With false indignation the masses try to cover up their own corruption and bad faith. They feel safer accusing others.

Another catastrophic legacy left to humanity by the Athens of Pericles was civil war. The Greek adolescent mind, in its inability to solve the problem of a pattern of life, produced a general fratricide, all Greeks killing each other in the name of abstract beliefs, nurtured by the demagogues. It was even considered heroic to kill one's friends and relations, and above all one's own progeny. Thucydides' description of the Greek Civil War illustrates this Greek legacy. "The ties of the party were stronger than the ties of blood: revenge was dearer than safety: the seal of good faith was not a moral law, but fellowship in transgressing it. Treacherous antagonism everywhere prevailed: for there was no word binding enough, no oath terrible enough to reconcile enemies. The leaders of either party used specious names, but all they wanted was power. They were carried away by senseless rage into the extremes of merciless cruelty and committed the most frightful crimes. Neither justice nor the public interest could set any limit to their revenges. The father slew the son, and the supplicants were dragged from the temples and slain."

In my view the Greek Civil War, as any civil war, was caused by adolescent fury at being unable to find a solution to the problem of organizing life on the level of self-infatuation. My view is strengthened by the following lines from Thucydides: "Reckless audacity is considered the courage of a loyal ally; prudent hesitation, specious cowardice, moderation, to be a cloak for unmanliness; the ability to see all sides of a question, a sign of incapacity to act on any. Frantic violence became the attribute of manliness. . . ." "The oath of reconciliation" was nothing but an expedient, "good as long as no other weapon was at hand; but, when opportunity offered, he who first ventured to seize it and to take his enemy off his guard, thought this perfidious revenge sweeter than an open one since, consideration of safety apart, success by treachery won him the palm of superior intelligence. Indeed it is generally the case that honest men are readier to call rogues clever than simpletons honest . . ."

What was "the cause of all these evils"?

"The lust for rule arising from greed and ambition," explained Thucydides.

Admirers of the Athens of Pericles will by now be shocked, ready to argue, "What about the Parthenon and the great Phidias?"

Pericles' policy ruined the agriculture industry, and Athens became a refuge for thousands of former landowners. These masses could not be kept merely by being paid or bribed as jurors, or with "liturgies" and festivals, although there were seventy various ceremonies a year in which the poor were fed free. In order to keep these masses calm and occupied, Pericles started public works with public money, and money from his allies. The monuments erected in this era were not inspired by Pericles' aesthetic sense, they were the needs of a demagogue. The Parthenon, and other Periclean monuments, although beautiful for some, are merely public works. To judge Pericles by the Parthenon is like judging Mussolini and Hitler by their auto routes.

In the end Pericles was brought before the court for the embezzlement of public funds. Phidias, Pericles' ally in public work, died in prison accused of stealing material and money given to him for statues.

Besides, one cannot judge a political system by artists of its period. Can the outrageous policies of the Borgias and Pope Julius II be judged by the works of Bramante, Michelangelo, Raphael, and Sansovino? Can the adventurous policy of Ludovico il Moro be judged by the works of his protégé, Leonardo da Vinci?

Most Greek tragedies can be attributed to the Greek *polis*, which a chain of political writers throughout history have glorified as the ideal form of state. The polis, however, was a necessity for the Greek adolescent male. He felt secure in a small, protected polis, secure in his self-infatuation.

Studying Greek history we gain the impression that civil wars and massive mutual killings were performed to save the polis from overpopulation, the polis only being able to exist with a limited number of citizens. Every Greek felt important in his small polis. In order to give every citizen a chance to become a member of the Council of the City State, there being a limited number of posts, no one was a councilor more than once and for more than a year. The polis was in character with the Greek adolescent.

In a small city-state everyone knew each other, everyone was a neighbor of the rest of the community. This was the price that the Greeks had to pay for their illusions of importance. Knowing each other so well nourished envy, jealousy, and antagonism. The vindictiveness of neighbors was the cause of strife and civil wars between the oligarchs and the democrats. There was little difference between the two parties, in any field of administration. There was no such difference, however, to justify either of the parties in joining the enemy of their polis in order to fight against its own city-state. It was in the nature of the polis, as it is in the nature today of any small community, to have two gangs fighting each other to kill. That the difference between the oligarchs and democrats was only an excuse for the extermination of local enemies can be deduced by the fact that often alliances of one group of a polis were made with their national or ideological enemies. The depth of hatred between the two gangs can be detected in the following description by Isocrates: "The owners of goods would prefer to throw them into the sea than to alleviate the misery of the poor, and the poor would be happy not so much as to take goods from the rich but to deprive the rich of these."

This Greek legacy to the world was particularly welcomed in Germany during their Thirty Years' War, where the Protestant states begged help from Catholic France in their fight against the Catholics who in turn were asking Protestant Sweden to help them.

In a society where women were treated so badly, it follows that work would be despised. Contempt for work was, in fact, another Greek legacy to mankind. "Work degrades men and makes them equal to animals," is a popular Neapolitan saying even today.

In Sparta, any manual work was considered degrading, but

"Every Greek felt important in his small polis."

idleness and leisure meant dignity and freedom. In Plutarch we read: . . . "this shows how much the Spartans considered any trade and handicraft base and servile." There was a law in Sparta forbidding citizens to work in any wage-earning trade.

In Plato's *Republic* we read: "It is fitting for a man to despise work." Plato's philosophy was that there should be an elite, an elite living in leisure. This was the only way to achieve wisdom.

To Aristotle "all manual works are without nobility; it is impossible to cultivate virtue and to live as a wage earner." In his *Politics* we read: "Wage earnings do not leave the mind either freedom or a chance of elevation." In Aristotle's view, leisure was necessary to "cultivate a virtuous soul, and to fulfil civic duties." He found nature generous because "it has produced a

THE MIND IN SEARCH OF A PATTERN   143

species of beings, slaves, who used their bodies to replace our fatigue."

According to Xenophon, Socrates said, "The workers and their handicraft are discredited and despised in the cities." . . . "With a weakened body, the mind weakens too. . . ."

In the third century B.C. we have evidence that even highly skilled work was considered undignified for a superman. Plutarch explained that Archimedes considered his engines and his technical inventions as merely "play for his geometry . . ." "He considered mechanics, and in general all artifacts, which are born out of need, as ignoble and base. . . ." Archimedes loved science, Plutarch explains, because "its beauty and its excellence have nothing to do with necessity."

The Fourth Century B.C.

At the beginning of the fourth century B.C., after the adolescent Greek mind had reduced the whole of Greece to economic ruin and moral chaos, a unique phenomenon occurred which became another Greek legacy: the glorification of madness, the same madness which had brought the ruin and chaos. In Plato's *Phaedrus* Socrates says: "Our greatest blessings come to us by way of madness. . . ." "Provided the madness is given by divine gift." With confusion of the mind, any madness becomes a "divine gift," "divine madness" or "sacred disease."

The Greeks interpreted any irrationality, even mental illness and abnormality, including epilepsy, as caused by the possession of some god, and therefore capable of inspiring luck—good or bad. Madness and abnormality began influencing human behavior. Through the practice of *defixiones*, even the dead were used to help the life of these Greeks unable to find a stable pattern of life.

The beginning of the fourth century B.C. in Greece was the perfect atmosphere for Philosophism, to use this expression invented by the French Encyclopedists. It was an atmosphere in which each individual mind was searching for an abstract or supernatural guideline for earthly life. Plato could only have been born into this atmosphere of Philosophism.

Plato invented a paradox of the human mind, a paradox which will be permanently repeated throughout history. (The word "paradox" is of Greek origin.) He started curing the confusion of the mind with the same mind which created the confusion. He wanted to solve the problem created by speculation, by increasing the speculation. This meant that to cure a physical illness, one had to make it worse. Plato thought that the only way to organize earthly life was to climb higher into transcendality.

In fact, through higher speculation in *The Republic*, Plato created an ideal state, a state suspended in the clouds of his imagination. This ideal state, however, could not solve the earthly pattern of life. It was too far removed from reality.

The ideal state created by the mind is known today, following the Thomas More term, as Utopia, meaning "nowhere." An even more appropriate name can be found in Aristophanes' satire *The Birds*. In this satire the birds are asked by two deluded citizens of Athens to build an ideal state, a polis in the air. All Utopias should be called "states in the air" or "cloud-states."

Plato only knew two kinds of standard men: one evil, the product of tyrannies, and one mediocre, the product of democracies. His ideal was a good standard man.

How did Plato's ideal state intend to produce a good standard man?

Platonically! After two years of military service, every single young citizen had to spend the next five years studying philosophy. The ruling class of Plato's ideal state was chosen from among the best philosophers, from those who had achieved clear ideas about the ideal entities: justice and goodness. This ruling class had to be above standard men. It had to consist of supermen. In Plato's view, this elite could only attain ideal entities through leisure and idleness, therefore living apart from economic and social reality. "Until philosophers are kings and kings philosophers there will be no salvation for states or the souls of men," he wrote.

With Plato's ideal state, an eternal question started: Who was to educate the educators of the ideal state? Modern Utopias answer this question by showing that the educators, in order to educate, do not have to be educated, just indoctrinated.

Plato claimed that all human behavior should be inspired by supreme good. What was this supreme entity that was supposed to direct human lives?

In the following letter, he admits that he has no idea: "There is no writing of mine on this subject, nor ever shall be. It is not capable of expression like other branches of study; but, as the result of long intercourse and a long time spent upon the thing, a light is suddenly kindled as from a leaping spark, and when it has reached the soul, it thenceforwards finds nutriment for itself." This supreme entity of Plato "was hard to find and impossible to describe to the masses," said Timaeus, a biographer of Plato. .

Cynical contempt of humanity, the common man in particular, is the main characteristic of all Utopians. At the entrance to his academy Plato wrote: "Let no one who is not a geometrician enter here."

That Utopians despise human beings can be deduced from the way humans are treated in Utopia: as inferior beings. The result of this is that all Utopias are despot governments or tyrannies. Plato's view was that man, being a "puppet," could easily adjust to the abstract idea of the ideal man, the man created in the mind of philosophers.

How was Plato's ideal state organized?

It was a church-state in which civil life was conducted as a religious performance. In this church-state, general abstract beliefs were fixed as laws of state, and imposed on the collectivity. Breakers of the law were punished. For minor offenses against the official state religion, the punishment was five years in a reformatory. Punishment for major offenses was banishment, solitary confinement for life in a particularly unhealthy or dangerous place, and death.

Intolerance toward ideas in contrast with official church-state doctrines, and its corollary, the persecution of heretics or "ideological enemies," was another of Plato's legacies to humanity. He was the first to discover ideological intolerance, the first to realize that the value of a belief was directly in proportion to its power to eliminate other beliefs with its monopoly, a word invented by the Greeks.

Plato's academy survived until the sixth century A.D., when, in the name of his own idea of persecution, it was closed down by

Justinian, to make room for a new official belief, Christianity, mainly inspired by Plato, through Neo-Platonism.

All Utopians, from Plato on, have had no sense of humor, therefore no sense of the ridiculous. They are prototypes of adolescents, always floating on a cloud of gloom. If Plato had had a sense of humor, he would have laughed at Aristophanes' satire *The Birds*, in which the humorous and ridiculous side of Utopias is shown.

The tragedy is that Plato has been used as a model by all other abstract speculators throughout history, speculators in search of an imaginary ideal state and an abstract pattern of life for male-dominated humanity. Only recently, after centuries of tragic and disastrous ventures by the human mind, are there signs of doubt that the mind can give or indicate a solution to the problem of finding a pattern of life. "With me the horrid doubt always arises as to whether the convictions of man's mind, which has been developed from the lower animal are of any value, or are at all trustworthy," wrote Darwin (from *Darwin's Life and Letters*, by Francis Darwin). H. G. Wells gives us a pathetic confession when, at the end of his life, he wrote *Mind at the End of Its Tether*, a book of great wisdom crammed into just thirty-two pages. We quote the following passages from it, hoping to put doubt into the minds of people who have faith in their mind: . . . "That sceptical mind may have overrated the thoroughness of its scepticism. As we are now discovering, there was still scope for doubting. The severer our thinking, the plainer it is that the dust-carts of Time trundle that dust off to the incinerator and there make an end to it. . . ." "Our world of self-delusion will admit none of that. It will perish amidst its evasions and fatuities." "Mind near exhaustion still makes its final futile movement towards that 'way out or round or through the impasse.' That is the utmost now that mind can do. And this, its last expiring thrust, is to demonstrate that the door closes upon us for evermore. There is no way out or round or through. . . ."

In 1932, Henri Bergson, in his *Les deux sources de la morale et de la religion*, claimed that Plato "in spite of 2,000 years of meditation about his ideas" did not advance our knowledge of ourselves one step. Bergson was right, not only as far as Plato was concerned, but as far as all philosophers are concerned, or anyone for that matter who pretends to solve the problem of earthly life by philosophizing about it. It is interesting to note that the philosophers hate each other, a clear evidence of the fragility of their worlds. For Schopenhauer, Fichte, Schelling, and Hegel were nothing but "the three sophists." "If I had my way," wrote Roger Bacon, "I would burn all the books of Aristotle, for the study of them can only lead to a loss of time, produce error, and increase ignorance."

For centuries men have considered women inferior beings, as they are incapable of being philosophers, or abstract thinkers. In fact, women find all philosophies laughable. Men's attitude is that of drug addicts. They consider those who do not take drugs as inferior.

With all the negative legacies that ancient Greece left humanity, she also left a positive one. The Greeks discovered the only solution for a mind at the end of its tether. When completely lost in his abstract thinking, the Greek male would go to Pythia in Delphi for advice, common sense and a touch of realism and reality.

Pythia of Delphi was well known, but each polis had its own Pythia, and sooner or later every Greek man ended up with his own personal Pythia in search of common sense.

With the Delphic Pythia, man's mind encountered the following irony. In order to enable men to accept her common sense, Pythia had to play their game, and pretend that her natural logic was inspired by a supernatural power; she had to pretend to be in a trance; she had to give the impression of being possessed by a deity, when giving advice. Man can never accept common sense in a simple way; he has to believe in it. To be accepted by man, common sense must be "inspired prophecy," given in an "ecstatic state."

Men believed in Pythia because they thought that she was possessed by a wise deity. At the same time they were aware that there was no wise deity in the Greek Pantheon, as Metis, the goddess of Wisdom, was swallowed by Zeus when she was pregnant.

Many writers consider that Pythia's wisdom was inspired by Apollo, Apollo being the protector of Delphic oracles. But was

MAN: THE FALLEN APE

Apollo really such a wise god? He committed one of the most unwise of deeds when he placed himself on the losing side on the Trojan War.

The divine madness of the fifth and the beginning of the fourth centuries B.C. produced economic misery. This misery can be seen in several plays of the period, and particularly in Aristophanes' *Plutus*.

STOICISM

The conceited Greek mind and its great achievement, demagogy, along with its champion, Demosthenes, the Athenian democratic leader, suffered a major defeat. In 338 B.C. at Chaeronea, Philip of Macedonia quelled the last Greek resistance and united Greece for the first time in her history.

The Greeks should consider their defeat at Chaeronea as beneficial to themselves and to mankind. It marked the end of an era. It was the destruction of the cradle of the Greek mind's self-infatuation, of the polis.

Philip of Macedonia and Alexander the Great put an end to city-states, in which every citizen was a king in his imagination. When the polis walls crumbled, the fresh air from the outside world cleansed the marketplace of its prejudices. With the empire of Alexander the Great, the Greek found himself part of the universe, instead of being the center of it. The Greeks found themselves lost in the wilderness of a new savannah.

Faced with the universe created by Alexander the Great, Greek men started to doubt the power of their mind, started retreating from their adolescent self-infatuation. The Greek male discovered woman. The cult of Cybele, the Great Mother of Asia Minor, and the cult of the Egyptian Isis, became popular.

Instead of the tragedies typical of the fifth and first half of the fourth centuries B.C., we have, with Philemon and Menander, the New Comedy era. In the New Comedy era, the Greek ceased to be static and egocentric. He moved, traveled and noticed others. Ordinary people with their everyday life were the themes of the comedies of the time.

With the new era, culture and science flourished. With culture, the Greeks discovered *logos;* through science they discovered the cosmos. Two schools expressed the new atmosphere: Epicureanism, and Stoicism. We will concentrate our attention mainly on Stoicism because of its important contribution to the grandeur of Rome, and particularly to the grandeur in the second century A.D. when Stoicism, the Roman Empire, and human civilization reached their peaks.

Human behavior should never be imposed by the mind, but by logos, by universal reason, the Stoics explained. Their attitude was "The sage lives in accordance with reason." "*Quid est ergo ratio?* [What is reason?]," Seneca asked himself. "*Naturae imitatio* [the imitation of nature]," he answered.

How can man embrace this attitude? By imitating woman's attitude to life. Any mature woman is a Stoic by nature. Stoic logic, a natural logic, is in its essence woman's logic; its precision and *simplicitas* is in contrast to man's logic, the logic of easy generalizations, approximations, assimilations, analogies, or hypotheses.

When the Greeks started preaching Stoicism, the Romans were already living as Stoics. This can be deduced by Lex Hortensia. This famous law of 287 B.C. emerged as a new way of creating laws: by *consensus bonorium,* through *plebiscitum.* We know that consensus is in woman's nature, and could only have been accepted as the source of laws in a culture influenced by woman. In man-dominated societies laws are imposed.

The Romans emphasized positive and active virtues such as magnanimity, benevolence, liberty and, above all, *humanitas.* Hadrian used *humanitas* with *felicitas* and *libertas* as the motto of the Empire. He illustrated the Roman meaning of humanitas on his coins. He was depicted raising a weeping woman to her feet.

The Roman's positive meaning of humanitas can be read in the following words repeated by Cicero and Terence: "*Homo sum, et nihil humani a me alienum puto,*" meaning, "I am a man therefore humanity is part of me." This is a feminine attitude. Woman's humanity is part of her nature, her instinct for the preservation of the species. Man, in his nature, is not humane; he can only either imitate woman's humanity or be guided by an abstract idea of it, which precludes from humanitas the opponents of his idea of it.

"*Any mature woman is a Stoic by nature.*"

"*We know that consensus . . . could only have been accepted as a source of laws in a culture influenced by woman.*"

"The other important Roman virtues were pietas, gravitas, *and* sublimitas."

The other important Roman virtues were *pietas, gravitas*, and *sublimitas*. These are attributes of the female nature.

What is the difference between a good deed inspired by the mind, and a good deed inspired by pietas and humanitas? In other words what is the difference between the good deed of a man and the good deed of a woman?

A man's good deed is the materialization of an abstract or religious idea of good. Man's good deed is a believer's good deed. The believer's good deed is never inspired by real need for good, but by his mind's need to do good.

Good deeds inspired by humanitas and pietas, woman's good deeds, are different. They start from outside, from the real need. The purpose of this good is to help the needy to their self-sufficiency, their dignity.

MAN: THE FALLEN APE

The following two sentences of Ovid explain the Roman meaning of virtue, an excellence in behavior dictated by intelligence, understanding, intuition, or common sense. *In medio stat virtus* and *Medio tutissimus ibis.* Virtue, for the Romans, was therefore in the middle, in between extremes. Exaggerated deeds, even if they were good deeds, produced negative effects in the eyes of the Romans. According to Tacitus they produced hatred and ingratitude.

Roman virtus was feminine in character. This is understandable if we take into consideration the following facts. Virtus comes from *vir* which means "man." Virtue, therefore, meant the behavior or attitude of a serious man. Who then defined the meaning of the word virtue? In a culture dominated by women, it will be the women who dictate what is virtuous, what the correct behavior is for the men.

There is some difficulty in understanding the Roman's real meaning of virtue, because the period of beliefs, which came after Rome collapsed, created believers' virtues or ideological virtues, which are a contradiction in terms. In belief, virtue means excess, simply because in beliefs, virtues are servile instruments of the beliefs.

Roman Justice

Stoicism helped the Romans to create their Jurisprudentia, a unique phenomenon in the history of mankind. It was a legal system based, "not on a theory but which came out of frequent conflicts and practical crises," as the historian Polybius explained.

Jus naturale, or *jus naturae* was based on the Stoic view of the open universe, of universally valid natural laws.

Jus gentium could have only been inspired by Stoic cosmopolitanism.

The famous Lex Aebutia of 150 B.C., which authorized Roman judges to overlook positive laws whenever *equitas*, reason or common sense required it, could only have been inspired by the Stoic cult of wisdom, by natural or universal reason.

Rome invented equitas and based her legal system on it. What was the real meaning of equitas?

It is difficult today to describe the real meaning of equitas, be-

"The cult of work . . ."

cause it died with Rome, and because since the fall of Rome humanity has only known man-made justice. Man's justice is a rigorous and codified justice. Its rigidity is justified by the consolation that it is equal for all. Man's justice is inspired by prejudices, abstract ideas, doctrines, beliefs, or infatuations. Equitas was justice without prejudices, justice without laws, and often it was justice against laws. In fact, this was the meaning of Lex Aebutia.

The following two sentences were the guidelines of the Roman judges: *Aequitas praefertur rigori*, meaning that equitas is preferable to rigorous laws, and *Aequitas de iure multum remittit* meaning that equitas softens laws.

Equitas was a Stoic virtue, and justice based on equitas was a supreme virtue. "*Iustitia omnium est domina et regina virtutum*," stressed Cicero in *De officiis*, calling justice the queen of virtues. Only by considering justice as the supreme virtue, can one understand the principle of Roman justice, of *Summum ius summa iniuria*, meaning that excessive rigor in justice creates injustice.

Work in Rome

Given the respect for woman in Rome, we may assume there was respect for work. In fact, Rome's greatness was built on respect for woman and the appreciation of work.

Around 700 B.C., during the reign of King Numa Pompilius, according to Plutarch, there were already *collegia*, professional corporations.

King Numa Pompilius gave land to all wishing to farm it, "even to the poorest of citizens," wrote Plutarch, "hoping that by bringing them out of their misery, to free them from their unfortunate necessity to commit evil deeds, and hoping that by leading a peaceful and healthy country life, these poor citizens would become more gentle, and hoping that in cultivating the land, they may cultivate themselves." King Numa Pompilius traveled around "to judge people by their work," Plutarch said. This wisdom, at the dawn of Rome's existence, is what made Rome's civilization the greatest ever known.

What kind of worker was the Roman?

He was conscientious and productive. This is shown in the following two sentences characteristic of Ancient Rome. "*Age quod agis*," Plautus suggests in his *Persa*; meaning, whatever you do, do it well. "*Aut non tentaris, aut perfice*," Ovid advises in his *Ars Amatoria*, meaning: Think before starting something, and if you start it, finish it. In work, more than in any other field, Roman gravitas was felt.

The cult of work can be deduced by the following line of Seneca in his *Epistulae Morales: "Nihil est quod non expugnet pertinax opera, et intenta ac diligens cure*," meaning that there is nothing that cannot be won with persistent work, and attentive and diligent care.

Work to Virgil was an instrument for the betterment of humanity. This great poet of nature expressed his optimism and confidence in his *Georgics* with the following words: "*Labor omnia vincit improbus*," meaning that hard work beats everything.

To Marcus Aurelius, work was the reason for one's existence.

The popular Roman proverb *Frater qui adiuvatur a fratre quasi civitas firma*, meaning that a strong city can be built with brother helping brother, shows us that the Romans were cooperative rather than competitive, which is, after all, in character with any society influenced by woman and her sense of organization. The co-operation went from the level of the *familia* to the level of the empire. The symbol of the empire was a bundle of rods tied together.

This co-operative division of labor produced specialized productions. Padua specialized in the production of linen, Rome in embroidery, Taranto, Potuoli, and Ancona in purple, Syracuse and Cunae in woolen goods. Judging by Pliny the Elder there were some candelabra of which the upper parts were made in the island of Aegina, and the lower in Taranto.

The transport of the goods by the *negociatores*, or tradesmen, from the production areas to the markets of the empire were facilitated by the great Roman roads. This network of roads is yet another proof that the economy leaned on co-operation. Greek

The via Flaminia, part of "this network of roads."

antagonism and competition, in economics, games and in life, never caught on in Rome, before the third century A.D.

But how, in practical terms, did this co-operation in Rome work? What was the power behind it?

The answer is *senioritas*. Based on age, the rule of seniority operated Roman co-operation, from Senate and magistracy to agriculture and trade. *Apex senectutis est auctoritas*, and Cicero in *De Senectute:* Senioritas and auctoritas went together in Rome. They inspired *reverentia* which was the incentive which operated in Roman society, based on co-operation. Respect for senioritas is more in the nature of women than in men.

Satires

Rome gave the world a new literary form, and a name to it. It was the satire of *satura*. In this literary creation we can find the specific characteristic of Roman culture. The Greeks gave us tragedies, tragedies mostly about woman; the Romans gave us *saturae*, satires mostly about men. These literary works represent two worlds: one dominated by men, the other by women. The Greeks depicted abstract and absurd characters and problems in tragic form; the Romans depicted real characters and problems in a humorous form.

Only a society which knew shame, a society where *pudor* existed, could have created saturae. Only in a society where man is in pre-adolescence, a stage in which maternal influence is still felt, can satires have a reason for existence, a real meaning.

In essence, the Roman satire was a maternal reaction to extreme attitudes or exaggeration in behavior. Scholars explain that the word satura comes from the Latin word *satur*, meaning a "medley" a "mixed stuffing," and "miscellany." In my view, the noun satura stems from the verb *saturare*, meaning that one has had enough, that one has reached saturation point. A satura is the reaction to saturation. It was the natural and spontaneous reaction in a shame culture. "Why do I write satires? Say, rather, how could I help it?" writes Juvenal in the introduction to one of his satires.

There are two main reactions to extreme attitudes and exaggeration in behavior: maternal and paternal. The paternal reaction is the order to stop extreme attitudes and exaggerations, the violent elimination of them and the punishment of those who exaggerated in order to give an example for the future. The paternal reaction is caused by provocation and so becomes a further exaggeration.

To a mother, any extreme behavior is merely a lack of common sense. The aim of her reaction is to awake common sense in the exaggerator, a sense of proportion and harmony. The only way to invoke common sense in someone who has lost it is to let him know that he has exaggerated. Women do it with humor, irony, mockery, jokes, and ridicule. In woman's view, man can stop exaggeration by eliminating it physically or by punishing those who exaggerate, but this does not establish common sense. *"Pudor si quim non flectit, non frangit timor,"* said Publius Siro, the Roman poet of the first century B.C., meaning that fear cannot break what shame cannot bend. That shame was an important break of extremes and exaggerations can be deduced by the following sentence of Seneca: *"Quod non vetat lex, hoc vetat fieri pudor,"* meaning that what is not forbidden by laws is forbidden by shame. Juvenal considered pudor the safest guideline in life when he said: *"Summum crede nefas animam praeferre pudori,"* meaning that big troubles are caused by preferring life to pudor.

That satura was held in high esteem in Rome, can be deduced by the fact that the great satirist Varro (116-27 B.C.) had his statue erected in the public library when he was still alive.

Roman satura was a creation of the Stoics. It was their reaction to the exaggeration of self-infatuation, of abstract speculations and absurd attitudes. The Romans were always suspicious of abstract speculations and Greek philosophizing. Lucian complained that the Romans preferred an "Alexandrian dancing master" to a "Greek philosopher." We can find the mockery of abstract speculations and sophistry in most of satires.

Juvenal criticized Greek philosophers and Jewish "professors of magic and prophecies" who were able to "sell you any dream you wanted for small change." The Greek will even seduce your grandmother, Juvenal claimed, if there was no one else available. "At any time of day or night a Greek is able to take his expression from another face," he wrote.

With the third century A.D., satura vanished from Rome. With the third century the Roman male entered the adolescent phase, the phase in which mockery was purposeless: there is no shame in adolescence. With Christianity, satura and satirists were persecuted.

Hygiene

The first move an animal makes after giving birth is to lick her offspring clean.

The cult of cleanliness is always prevalent in societies influenced by women. A peculiarity of Rome, which illustrates Roman culture, was the *thermae*, the baths.

The thermae of the Roman Empire were not just reserved for the privileged. Agrippa made the thermae free, and bath oils were gifts from the emperors. At the beginning of Christianity there were about 11 large public baths in Rome, and 856 smaller ones. Some, such as the baths of Caracalla and the baths of Diocletian, had about 5,000 visitors a day, and could hold 1,600 people at the same time.

One of the first things that the Christians destroyed were the thermae, and after a few centuries of Christianity Rome had not one public bath.

The Romans gave more importance to hygiene than any other peoples before or since. The Roman motto *Mens sana in corpore sano* could only have been maternal advice.

Hygeia, the goddess of cleanliness, was worshiped as much as Aesculapius, the god of medicine. Her name was mentioned with that of Hippocrates in the oath of medical professions. "We can therefore conceive Stoicism as a spiritual hygiene," wrote Schopenhauer in his *The World as Will and Idea.*

It should be emphasized that the Romans considered the baths natural and kept them for physical necessity, without transforming them into a pleasure. This can be deduced from the following sentence of Seneca in his *Epistolae: "Curam nobis nostri natura mandavit; sed huic ubi nimium, indulseris, vitium est,"* meaning that nature demands care of the body, but that any exaggeration of it is a vice.

"The cult of cleanliness . . ."

"The fall of Rome must have been caused by the erosion of these pillars."

THE DECLINE AND FALL OF ROME

Rome's greatness was built on the enthusiasm of the Romans in the stage of their pre-adolescence, on Stoicism which appealed to woman's gravitas, on the respect for women and on the respect for work. If my thesis is correct, the fall of Rome must have been caused by the erosion of these pillars.

Any unbiased historian knows that history has never recorded a better world before or since the second century A.D. in Rome.

Here I would like to quote the opinion of two great experts on this period: Gibbon and Mommsen.

"If a man were called to fix the period in the history of the world during which the condition of the human race was most happy and prosperous," wrote Gibbon in his *Decline and Fall of the Roman Empire*, "he would, without hesitation, name that which elapsed from the death of Domitian to the accession of Commodus" (A.D. 96–180). "The vast extent of the Roman Empire was governed by absolute power, under the guidance of virtue and wisdom. The armies were restrained by the firm and gentle hand of four successive emperors, whose characters and authority commanded involuntary respect. The forms of the civil administration were carefully preserved by Nerva, Trajan, Hadrian, and the Antonines, who delighted in the image of liberty, and were pleased with considering themselves as the accountable ministers of the laws."

Mommsen, in his *Provinces of the Roman Empire* writes: "Even now there are various regions of the East, as of the West, as regards which the imperial period marks a climax of good government, very modest in itself, but never withal attained before or since; and, if an angel of the Lord were to strike the balance whether the domain ruled by Severus Antoninus was governed with the greater intelligence and the greater humanity at that time or in the present day, whether civilization and national prosperity generally have since that time advanced or retrograded, it is very doubtful whether the decision would prove in favor of the present."

One could accuse Gibbon and Mommsen of being nostalgic, but we have a contemporary comment about the same period lauding the present, one of the rarest things for humans. Aelius Aristidas (A.D. 129–81) described the second century A.D. on the following lines: "The whole world seems to be in a festive mood; people have discarded their old garb, which was of iron, to give themselves in full liberty to the beauties and the joy of living. All the cities have renounced their old rivalries, or rather they are all animated by the same emulation: to present themselves as the most beautiful, the most delectable. Everywhere we see gymnasia, fountains, propylaea, temples, workshops, schools."

The great enigma which has intrigued scholars for centuries is

"*A chain of historians accepted Voltaire's explanation that Christianity 'opening the heavens, lost the empire.'*"

"*With the adolescent revolution in Rome came ambition and pretentiousness . . .*"

why this glorious Rome of the second century A.D. collapsed in the fifth century after having survived the agony and confusion of the third and fourth centuries. Many attributed the fall of Rome to Christianity. Voltaire's explanation that Christianity, "opening the heavens, lost the Empire," was accepted by a chain of historians.

Christianity existed in the first and second century and it was not considered a serious matter. Judging by Marcus Aurelius, Christianity was "sheer obstinacy," greatly despised by the majority of Romans. Why then did Christianity only become popular at the end of the third century? Some historians attribute the reason for the fall of Rome to the barbarians and their invasions, but the barbarians had existed long before without being a threat. The Roman answer to the problem was Caesar's *Veni, vidi, vici.*

Then what happened?

By the end of the second century, and the beginning of the third century the Roman male had passed from pre-adolescence into full adolescence. It was in that period that the adolescent revolution in Rome began.

This new stage in Roman history was accompanied by the following characteristics of male humanity: self-infatuation inspired by the courage to lean on abstract beliefs of the mind, contempt for women and their gravitas, the only way to overcome shame, and despise of work.

The start of the trend of self-infatuation, arrogance, and, above all, the worship of physical strength, was illustrated by the new title of Emperor Commodus (180–93). He called himself Hercules Romanus. It is also characteristic of the new era that Commodus was killed when impersonating a gladiator, the killer's name, Narcissus, reflecting the new atmosphere too. Mitra, this Indo-Iranian male deity, this "warrior" and "victorious god," this *sol invictus,* attracted the most arrogant element of Roman adolescence.

The adolescent revolution was spurred on by Caracalla's Constitutio Antoniana of A.D. 212. This gave Roman citizenship to all freeborn inhabitants of the empire, and a large number of the new citizens became filled with self-importance. History teaches us that increase of rights or privileges weakens the sense of duty, personal responsibility, and readiness for sacrifice. With full rights, any sacrifice becomes a humiliation.

With the adolescent revolution in Rome came ambition and pretentiousness, which, as in any other adolescent revolution, brought anarchy in which the law of the stronger became the only rule. This atmosphere is best illustrated by the fact that in the second century there were only five emperors, while in the third century and from the death of Commodus in 193 to the arrival of Diocletian in 284, there were among the legitimate and illegitimate emperors, as many as there were years. Lactantius (240–320) in his *De mortibus Persecutorum* (c. 318), stressed that soon "there will be more governors than governed." He was criticizing Diocletian who, in order to satisfy the new wave of wanting to command, had inflated the civil service and the army.

At the middle of the third century, the insecure mediocrity, the main victim of the disorder in which the stronger dominated the weaker, slowly started to revert to a father-protected infancy, the strong, omnipotent Christian father. Christianity promised them a privileged position in the next world, it promised them immortality. What is more, it threatened punishment in hell to the successful, the fitter and the stronger, the envied.

This lost mediocrity discovered abstract thinking, the Greek philosophy. (Previously Greek philosophers had been a mocking stock, often expelled from Rome.) This increased even more the contempt for the work, and the enthusiasm for Christianity. Christianity glorified idleness—passivity was a virtue. The Christians considered work a punishment for original sin.

It is interesting to note the origin of the word *Pagani*, pagans. Today it means non-Christian. Originally it meant working people from villages. With Christianity it became an expression of contempt, a derogatory term for the working people. In the agricultural industry, where woman's influence was felt more strongly, work remained more highly esteemed than in towns or in other industries. Female deities of agriculture remained worshiped long after Christianity took full power.

With the first Christian communities, St. Paul was in fact faced with a serious problem of laziness among the members. We see this from his epistles addressed to the Community of Thessalonica. He was so disappointed by life in the first communities that he proclaimed, "Who does not work has no right to eat." (When the Russians formed their Communist State in 1917, after many unhappy vicissitudes, brought about by idleness, their leaders fixed, in Article 12 of their Constitution of 1936, still in vigor, the following rule for Soviet society: "Work in the USSR is the duty of every citizen able to work, following the principle: 'Who does not work, does not eat.'")

Greek ideas about work, particularly those of Plato and Aristotle, became popular with the Romans in their adolescent phase. Plotinus, who launched Neoplatonism in Rome, considered work "a shadow of contemplation," and the main obstacle to his doctrine of ecstasy, to the elevation of the mind. *Ex-stasis* meant for Plotinus and his times a state outside reality, a life without any responsibility. Plotinus started the fashion for hermits and vagabonds.

The glorious Roman roads, now served only vagabonds or military gangs, the former in search of alms, the latter of power and pillaging.

There was a pathetic appeal to work by the Emperor Septimius Severus, the successor of Commodus, who, with the help of the learned jurist Papinian, tried desperately to reverse the rising tide of the adolescent revolution. His dying message to the empire was: *Laboremus* (Let us work!). It was the plea of someone who felt that the era whose motto was *Ego, ergo ago*, meaning that the dignity of ego implied work, was over forever.

In many books we read that with the coming of Christianity, work began to be honored. This is not true! We have seen the high esteem for work in pre-Christian Rome. I have also mentioned St. Paul's efforts to force the first Christians to work. Life in monasteries before the reform of Benedict of Nursia (sixth century) and the reform of Colomban (seventh century) gives us the sad picture of idleness and contempt for work among the Christians. For the Christians, work was always an expiation.

Work lost its value and esteem with the fall of Rome, and only started regaining them in the nineteenth century in North America.

I must now explain why fallacies concerning pre-Christian Rome are still part of Western belief. The answer can be found in the fact that the teaching of ancient history has for centuries been the monopoly of the Christian Church.

The Christian Church explained *Pro domo sua*, the past. It was explained in the way that suited the Church. It was all started by St. Augustine of Hippo with his dangerous legacy to the world, his so-called *Philosophy of History*. Between 415–17 St. Augustine gathered around him Orosius and other learned Christians with the purpose of writing a history of the past from the Christian point of view, for Christian use. The main idea was to denigrate pre-Christian Rome, emphasizing the negative side of ancient Roman life. In fact their work was called *Historiae adversum Paganos*, stories against Pagans.

The adaptation of the past to the needs of the present, started by Christianity, was followed by other religions and ideologies. It has now become a part of the spiritual patrimony of mankind.

One might ask oneself whether St. Augustine was to blame when he changed the facts of history, or was it the people who wanted to be deceived. Why did the leaders of Christianity in the first and second centuries not succeed where St. Augustine and St. Ambrose did? One has the impression that the people at a certain moment wanted to be seduced by fallacies. The Roman cardinal Carlo Caraffa said to the religious or political leaders: "*Vulgus vult decipi, ergo decipiatur* [the masses wanted to be deceived, therefore let them be deceived]."

When Christianity came to power, the Christians adapted every thing to their way of thinking. They kept the same terminology for many things, simply perverting their meaning. With Christianity, Roman virtue became a religious virtue which, as I have already stated, is a contradiction in terms.

The Roman auctoritas, the moral influence, became Christian auctoritas, dogma, the dogmatic influence. Roman humanitas became Christian humanity, meaning the persecution of non-Christians. In fact the victory of Christianity marked the end of religious tolerance in the Roman world. With Christianity, *amor dei* became *timor dei*.

St. Augustine gave a new meaning to *sapientia*. It was no

longer knowledge and understanding of reality, but a mystical state of mind. It was becoming part of *le milieu divin*, an expression so dear to Pierre Teilhard de Chardin.

Pietas became Christian pietas, an abstract idea serving an abstract religion.

Justice was no longer a virtue, it was no longer guided by equitas. With Justinian, justice was codified in his Corpus Juris Civilis. The Justinian code kept the same terminology and the same laws of Ulpianus, Paulus, and Papinianus, but it had a different meaning and a different interpretation. Roman law served the people. With Christianity, the people served the law, and the law served the Christian doctrine. With Christianity judges are watched, and judged too by the office of the Holy Spirit.

Prudentia or *providentia*, wisdom shown in the exercise of judicious forethought, became providence with the Christians, or the divine guidance of a lost and frightened being. It had to keep hope and faith alive, the supreme virtues of the Christian Church.

With Christianity, Roman equality became an equality of sinners; what is more, of sinners responsible for an inherited sin. The paradoxical idea of inherited sin, inspired the paradoxical law of the Christian Emperor Arcadius, which punished even the children of a guilty parent, guilty of crimes against the State, the Christian State.

Charity, which in Rome contrasted with *dignitas* and *sublimitas*, became a Christian virtue which encouraged idleness and "contemplation."

The Christians painted a distorted picture of the Roman familia. It was distorted to serve the Christian idea of a family dominated by the father.

Every scholar agrees that the Romans, before the Neoplatonism of the third century, were disinclined to be seduced by abstract thinking. If this is so, then we must accept that Roman men had nothing to lean on in their behavior but maternal common sense. Without abstract thinking, the Romans could have had no ideas of their own on which to base their behavior.

We know that the familia was the center of Roman life. The familia was a typical Roman institution which died with Rome. It cannot be equated with the family in the modern sense, the family created by Christianity. Familia was an institution which embraced the family in the strict sense, slaves, *clientes* and above all, the *lares* and *penates*, the cult of the dead and the cult of the deities of the familia.

The Roman familia was a *mater familias* institution. It had existed in Rome from prehistoric times. With the evolution of time the mother slowly became physically substituted by the *pater familias*, who continued to exercise the functions inherited by the mater familias. He exercised his functions in the way a mother would have done.

Bachofen, in his *The Right of the Mother*, explained that Rome had a promiscuous life in her prehistory. In that period, judging by Cicero's words in his *De inventione*, "No one knew of lawful marriage, no one had seen legitimate children of his own." Out of this promiscuity, Bachofen explained, emerged matriarchy and then patriarchy. This patriarchy, in Rome, must have been an imitation of matriarchy. The real patriarchy came with Christianity when the pater familias assumed an abstract role dictated to him by the Almighty God, the Father. Only an abstract idea like Almighty could have inspired an abstract role like the omnipotent father in the family. In the human species the omnipotent pater familias is not a natural phenomenon but an invention of religions dominated by an Only and Almighty God.

We have been taught that the pater familias, with his patria potestas, dominated the Roman familia like an unscrupulous despot. We are also told that the life or death of the members of his family depended on his mood.

But was this really so? Or was it invented by Christian scholars in order to justify the medieval pater familias, the feudal, ruthless, barbarian despot? Was the Roman pater familias really that absolute ruler?

Christianity depicted the Roman pater familias to suit her cause. Christianity decided to build her empire on the family. This Christian microcosm had to be ruled by the same rules as the Christian macrocosm, by Almighty God. The pater familias of the Christian family, or of any family in any culture which is dominated by an almighty male deity, is an abstract creation molded on the image of the Supreme God—the Supreme God created by man's mind. In this highly artificial position of the

Christian pater familias, one can find the source of men's neuroses, increasing with the liberation of women.

First of all, there are very few cases of the Roman pater familias killing members of his family in the name of patria potestas. The last known case was in 65 B.C. when Aulus Fulvius was killed by his father when he was discovered participating in the Catiline conspiracy. But his father obtained the permission of the Roman Senate before doing this.

Above the pater familias there was a domestic council composed of the main members of the family which in reality, decided any question concerning the familia. It must be stressed that whenever there was a decision to be taken about the wife, her kith and kin had to be a part of the domestic council.

Above the pater familias there was that important institution in Roman life, Censorius. Through this important Roman institution of censorship, public opinion exercised its power. The spirit of the famous Cato the Censor dominated Roman life until the end of classical Rome. He received the place of honor from Virgil in *The Aeneid* and from Dante in his *Divina Commedia*.

The pater familias, in exercising his patria potestas was specially influenced and guided by the spirit of the household deities. The guardian and interpreter of the spirit of the household deities was the Roman *matrona*. Through her interpretation of these spirits, dreams, and omens, the Roman matrona exercised influence over her husband. Classical Rome emphasized the stupidity of Caesar in not listening to the advice of his wife, Calpurnia, when she told him not to go to the Senate on the Ides of March.

Many writers, influenced by the Christian interpretation of Roman life, explain that the wife in the Roman familia was an object at the disposal of her husband; that she was *in manu mariti*, under his total power. These writers failed to point out that this form of marriage was already in disuse by the third century B.C. Roman marriage, the most solemn moment in their lives, was the union of two free wills, based on *affectio maritalis*—mutual respect. The marriage lasted as long as the mutual respect lasted. We read in W. G. de Burgh's *The Legacy of the Ancient World*, the following: "As time went on, the advance of public opinion, the gradual disuse of the old forms of marriage which placed the bride in her 'husband's hand,' (manus), and the introduction of new methods of evading the law of tutelage, combined to secure for Roman women a freedom and independence hardly paralleled in ancient or modern society."

Cicero's sentence in *De officiis: "Prima societas in ipso conjugio est,"* meaning the first society is marriage, can only make sense if the woman is free and independent, before, during, and after marriage.

Scholars interpret the famous words, *Quando tu Caius, ego Caia,* pronounced by women concluding marriage by Confarreatio, as an agreement of the wife to blindly follow her husband for better or for worse. It was not in the nature of Roman women to follow any man blindly. Taking into consideration the freedom of the Roman woman and her dominance in Roman life, the above sentence accompanying the marriage can only have one meaning: admonition by the wife to the husband. It is "as long as you behave like a good husband, I will be a good wife." Roman history is filled with examples of wives ceasing to behave like Caia when the husband was not behaving like Caius, meaning with dignitas and auctoritas.

The Roman matrona was the real domina of the familia and was addressed by this title by all members of the family including the husband. "Before the Roman matron, nothing could be said which was disgraceful, nothing could be done which was dishonourable," stressed Tacitus in his *Dialogue on Oratory*.

A Roman woman, dressed in her *stola matronalis*, took precedence and inspired respect. Even the Praetorian guard bowed to a pregnant domina.

The position of women in Roman life is best explained by the famous sentence of Cato the Elder: "All nations ruled their wives, we rule all nations, but our wives rule us."

As far as adultery is concerned, we have seen that a husband had the right to kill his adulterous wives in male-dominated cultures, as in Mesopotamia and Israel. In Greece, Draco authorized the offended man to kill the adulterer of even his sister or his mother. He deprived a man of citizenship if he forgave the adultery of his wife. In Rome, before Lex Julia (18 B.C.), adultery was a private affair judged by the domestic council of the family or by Quaestio, a special court presided over by the Praetor in cases when the domestic council could not agree. With Lex Julia, the Praetor was authorized to inflict on adulterers, *relegatio*, permanent or temporary banishment. As soon as Christianity was in power, the Draconian laws were reapplied to adulterers; they were sentenced to death. In ancient Rome, a non-married woman was freer in her sexual behavior than ever before or since.

One of the reasons why the Roman matrona held such power was that her husband was seldom at home. He was either in the Forum, or the thermae, or in administration in the provinces, or he was at war. The Roman matrona was the real administrator of the household.

The Roman matrona's great influence over Roman life, lay in the fact that it was she who was in charge of the education of the children, choosing their tutors. Here we can understand why Stoicism was so successful in Rome. The Stoics were the Roman matrons' favorite teachers. Their attitudes and their teachings were in accordance with the matrona's way of life. Greek philosophers, or preachers of abstract philosophies, were despised by Roman women. When they were employed by Roman families they were treated as servants by the matronae, Lucian, a Greek philosopher, complained in his *Nigrinus*. Often, wrote Lucian, the Greek philosophers had to carry the matrona's dog, who "licked his beard and peed on his cloak." Lucian also complained that Roman matronas, before taking a Greek into service, would thoroughly investigate his background, views, and references, and even invite him to a grand feast to see what his table manners were like.

The women of ancient Rome were always respected. Following one of the most popular legends, Rome's independence started with the virtue of Lucretia, the model wife of Tarquinius Collatinus.

We meet the glorification of the independence and freedom of Roman woman in the story of Virginia, told by Dionysius of Halicarnassus. Her father preferred to kill her than give her to a rich man, who was infatuated by her beauty, against her will. "My child," said Virginia's father, stabbing her to death, "I send you free and chaste to your ancestors in the world of the dead; for while you live the tyrant allows you to have neither freedom nor chastity."

MAN: THE FALLEN APE

Livy tells the story of Veturia who, when she heard that her son Coriolanus was at the doors of Rome with an army of Volsci, enemies of Rome, intending to occupy the city, went to see him in his camp and saved Rome, addressing her son with the following words: "Tell me, before I accept your embrace, whether I have come to see my son or an enemy, whether I am your prisoner or your mother in this camp" . . . "When you came in sight of Rome, did you not think, within these walls are my home and my household gods, my mother, my wife and my children? If I had never been a mother, Rome would not now be suffering the attack of an enemy; if I had no son, I would have died a free woman in a free country." This happened about 491 B.C.

We know that girls were given the same education as boys. The only exception was that girls were not taught rhetoric. It may have been for practical reasons, judging by Juvenal's explanation that rhetoric was insufficient for a livelihood.

There have never been, before or since the days of ancient Rome, so many outstanding women. Cornelia influenced her sons, Gaius Gracchus and Tiberius Gracchus. Her house at Misenum was a meeting place for learned people, including Cicero. Sempronia was an influential ally of Catiline. Caesar was influenced by his mother, Aurelia. Augustus owes his greatness to the education he received from his mother, Atilia, and to the help and understanding of his wife, Livia. Everyone knows the influence exercised on Nero by his mother, Agrippina, and by his mistress and subsequent wife, Poppaea. Tiberius had to move to Capri in order to escape from the influence of his mother, Livia, and her powerful *salon*. Caracalla was dominated by his mother, Julia Domna. Mark Antony, judging by Plutarch, allowed his wife, Fuliva, "to rule a ruler and to command a commander."

From St. Augustine on, one of the means of denigrating Roman civilization by Christian writers has been by stressing the cruelty of Roman games. Actually Roman games were inspired by the Stoic attitude toward death. Stoicism attempted to liberate man from his hysteric fear of death, preaching that death should be faced with dignity and equanimity. Seneca was clear when he said, "*Qui mori didicit, servire dedicit,*" meaning that those who do not fear death will never become slaves, that only by liberating oneself from the fear of death can one live a life of true freedom and dignity.

The collapse of the Roman Empire began with the collapse of the Roman familia, the stronghold of the empire, caused by the adolescent revolution. Christianity helped the destruction of the Roman familia by the attack on its backbone—woman. The strongest weapon in the hands of Christianity in denigrating women was its emphasis on Eve's responsibility for the lost paradise. "You destroyed so easily God's image, man," was the motto of Christianity in their policy of the denigration of woman. Christianity also started denigrating women by emphasizing the myth that she was created from one of man's ribs.

"Every woman should be ashamed of the thought that she is a woman," was early Christianity's attitude.

In the end Christianity succeeded in destroying the Roman familia, replacing it with the Christian family in which the woman was reduced to being her husband's slave.

We read in the Ephesians the following:

Wives, submit yourselves unto your own husbands, as unto the Lord.
For the husband is the head of the wife, even as Christ is the head of the church: and he is the savior of the body.
Therefore as the church is subject unto Christ, so let wives be to their own husbands in everything.

The status of women in Rome changed radically in nine centuries. ". . . and three kings, namely Tatius, the elder Tarquin, and Servius Tullius, were succeeded by their sons-in-law. . . . Thus it would seem that among Aryan people, at a certain stage of their social evolution, it has been customary to regard woman, and not man, as the channels through which royal blood flows," wrote J. G. Frazer in *The Golden Bough*. But with Christianity, the notion of *Genio urbis Romae, sive mas sive femina* (To the genius of Rome be it male or female) disappeared.

Only in 1950 the Catholic Church officially raised to "heavenly glory," the "Immaculate Mother of God, the ever Virgin Mary." The Protestant attitude towards women is still based on the teachings of Martin Luther in his *Vindication of Married Life* where he writes: ". . . man is higher and better than she; for the regiment and dominion belong to man as the head and master of the house as St. Paul says elsewhere: Man is God's honor and God's image. Item: Man does not exist for the sake of woman, but woman exists for the sake of man and hence there shall be this difference, that a man shall love his wife but never be subject to her, but the wife shall honor and fear the husband."

CHRISTIANITY

With the victory of Christianity most of Europe reverted to man-made infancy, protected by Almighty God the Father. The last two creations of the mind were: The Credo and the Church. The Church's reason for existence was "to compel men to salvation" . . . "to bring them to God," as St. Augustine claimed. These creations of the mind became a patrimony of humanity. The present Soviet Church with its Brezhnev doctrine which allows the Russians to "compel Czechoslovaks to salvation," is evidence that the human mind has been unable to produce any new guideline for human behavior.

Christianity transformed belief, an abstract creation of the mind, into a supreme virtue.

"I believe in God, the Father almighty, Creator of heaven and earth. And in Jesus Christ, His only Son, Our Lord, who was conceived by the Holy Ghost, born of the Virgin Mary, suffered under Pontius Pilate, was crucified, dead and buried: He descended into hell, the third day He rose again from the dead. He ascended into heaven, and sitteth at the right hand of God the Father almighty, from thence He shall come to judge the living and the dead. I believe in the Holy Ghost, the Holy Catholic Church, the Communion of Saints, the forgiveness of sins, the resurrection of the body, and life everlasting. Amen."

A belief in absurdities which are contrary to the most obvious laws of nature, is what the human mind achieved, and what is more, became proud of. Belief has become a part of humanity, the opium of the people. What changes occasionally is the object of the belief—the absurdity.

*"Christianity transformed belief,
an abstract creation of the mind,
into a supreme virtue."*

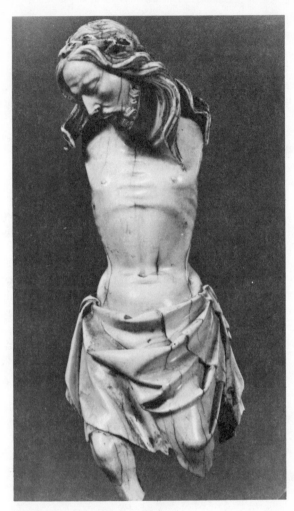

*"A belief in absurdities which
are contrary to the most obvious
laws of nature. . . ."*

There have been several revolutions trying, in the name of the rational, to liberate humanity from beliefs. These revolutions have ended consistently either with an intensification of the belief, or with a change of the object of the belief. The Renaissance reinforced Christianity through Protestantism and Counter-Reformation. Rationalism of the seventeenth century merged into the Romanticism of the eighteenth century which brought the human mind to a degree of exaltation and poetic illusions never seen before in history. The scientific revolution of the nineteenth century produced "scientific socialism," a contradiction in terms.

The French Revolution produced Napoleon, and Napoleon, after having played like a naughty boy with the world, finished by saying: "*La politique est la fatalité*." No one mocked humanity better than Victor Hugo when, after the Battle of Waterloo, he wrote: "If it had not rained during the night of 17–18th June, 1815, the future of Europe would have been different. Napoleon was overthrown by a few drops of water." Something must be seriously wrong with a species whose whole life can be radically changed by a few drops of rain.

I would like to illustrate this point with a fictitious dialogue between the last Czar of Russia and Stalin when they met in heaven:

Czar: Tell me, how is life in Russia now? Is the almighty Father of all Russians still in the Kremlin?

Stalin: Yes.

Czar: Is there still only one belief dictated by the Kremlin?

Stalin: Yes.

Czar: Do you compel disbelievers to follow the official belief of the Kremlin?

Stalin: Yes.

Czar: Do you forbid the people to read anything that is not in accordance with the official state doctrines, as we did?

Stalin: Yes.

Czar: Do you send mad people like writers and intellectuals who dare to criticize in the name of reason the official belief, to Siberia or exile, as we did?

MAN: THE FALLEN APE

Stalin: Yes.

Czar: Do you still produce that wonderful vodka at 63 proof?

Stalin: No! We now have vodka at 65 proof.

Czar: Was the revolution really worth while for just two extra degrees of alcohol?

Among the main victims of belief were the Jewish people. For two thousand years they awaited their God to prepare Israel for them. After two thousand years they discovered the Roman Stoic advice, *Dei facientes adiuvant*, meaning that gods help those who help themselves.

Men continue to build their pattern of life on beliefs. In nature if anything has to be built it has to start from the earth, from reality, because of the law of gravity. The foundations of belief are never on earth, they are always in the clouds, in transcendentality. Any time humans build a belief, they do it upside down. It might be considered funny if it did not cost so many lives and such a lot of resources spent in vain.

Judging by man's readiness blindly and happily to follow absurd beliefs, one deduces that the peculiarity of human males is that they love to suffer, that they love to complicate each other's lives. The religious and political leaders, knowing this, treat humanity in the only way they really like to be treated—with disdain. The religious and political leaders, in order to be successful, learned how to treat people from that successful politico-religious leader Cardinal Richelieu. In his *Testament Politique* (1642) the Cardinal gave the following message:

"If the people were too comfortable it would be impossible to keep them within the rules of their duties. If they were free of tributes they would assume to be also free of obedience. One must compare people with mules, who, being accustomed to heavy loads, would be more easily spoilt by rest than by hard work."

"Aggression . . . is really an essential part of the life-preserving organization of instincts." Konrad Lorenz.

PART FOUR

Aggression

In spite of many writers dedicating pages to the subject of aggression, there is still confusion about the origin and nature of aggression. In his book *On Aggression*, Konrad Lorenz wrote: "Summing up what has been said in this chapter, we find that aggression, far from being the diabolical, destructive principle that classical psychoanalysis makes it out to be, is really an essential part of the life preserving organisation of instincts." This contradicts another idea of Lorenz's, stressed in the same book, that humans are "specialists in non-specialisation," opportunists. By definition, opportunists cannot have an instinct of aggression.

Freud, after having based all his specific works on instincts at the end of his life wrote the following: "The theory of instincts is, so to speak, our mythology. Instincts are mythical entities, magnificent in their indefinitiveness. In our work we cannot for a moment disregard them, yet we are never sure that we are seeing them clearly."

But what is even more confusing, is that most books that supposedly deal with human aggression, deal in fact, with animal aggression. They conclude syllogistically that as animals have instincts of aggression, and as humans are animals, humans therefore also possess the instinct of aggression. Some authors go so far as to claim that aggression is beneficial because it ensures peace and order in the human community and because it succeeds in ensuring peace and order in the community of "hens and ducks in Norway."

Even if these writers could establish some similarity between human and animal aggression, they still have no explanation for gang aggressions, for human social and international conflicts. In the animal world the fight is usually between individuals.

Here I must stress again that in the animal world, particularly in intra-specific conflicts, there is more of a ritualized game, or even an elegant dance, than a real fight, the game being composed of the threat, the display of strength, the submission, or the flight of one of the antagonists. Flight is the general rule in nature, with fight as the exception, occurring only when flight is impossible. Lethal intra-specific fight is an accident, even between carnivorous predators.

In *Man and Aggression,* Ashley Montagu was right when he stressed the following: "It seems rather hard on animals to project the failings of mankind upon them, and to blame them for having bequeathed those failings to us."

I must add, however, that there is some similarity in behavior between domestic animals and humans. They are both dependent and insufficient beings. Like humans, domestic animals must have originated from the omega individuals of their species. With domestication an animal enters an artificial environment, created by humans. In artificially created environments domesticated animals become opportunists. Pavlov's theory of conditioned reflexes could have never been valid with a wild dog or a self-sufficient wolf. Pavlov's dogs, in their nonself-sufficiency, have no choice but to adapt themselves, to accept the game of conditioned reflexes imposed on them by those upon whom they depend for survival.

The same game of conditioned reflexes is valid with humans when they are reduced to the level of Pavlov's dogs, when humans find themselves completely dependent on an authority for their survival. The game is over, however, as soon as humans, or dogs, are no longer dependent for survival on the authority who plays the game, or when life is in immediate danger. Pavlov's dogs lost their acquired conditioned reflexes after their lives were threatened with the sudden flood of the river Neva. Conditioned or indoctrinated humans will do likewise when faced with a catastrophe.

To behaviorists, the aggression of a human being, as any other human behavior, "is controlled by genetic and environmental histories," we read in *About Behaviorism* by B. F. Skinner. This is a very useful theory for man who likes to blame external circumstances for his capricious behavior.

The extreme difference between the biological and sociological, or the ethological and psychological approach to human aggression is due, in my view, to an aggressive approach to the problem of aggression. One has the impression that aggression is one of those subjects with the power to inspire extreme attitudes in those who decide to study it. One of the most curious of these extreme attitudes has been achieved by a school of writers who explain that there is no intra-specific aggression in the human species because the aggressor does not usually consider his victims as human beings. By this theory, the Nazi's extermination of the Jews and Slavs cannot be considered an intra-specific aggression. Nazis did not consider their victims as human beings.

The confusion in the field of human aggression is also caused by the fact that most scientists do not deal with man and woman separately, and above all they do not separate Homo sapiens from man in the woodlands or man in the savannah. According to the majority of writers, the human species in the savannah was aggressive simply because modern man is aggressive.

In my view, there are two different aggressions: natural or rational aggression, and supernatural or irrational aggression. The former can be offensive and defensive. Offensive aggression is found in male animals in their intra-specific fights for sexual selection, and in their inter-specific fights, their protection of the species. Defensive aggression is found in all animals, and in human females. Natural aggression is based on instinct. Supernatural aggression is caused by the mind and its creations, beliefs, self-infatuation, and arrogance. This typically man-made aggression started with the discovery of the mind. This aggression is unique in nature. It has no limits or rules. It is unpredictable.

Man is not aggressive by nature, he has no instinct of aggression; man is aggressive by supernature; supernature puts man in conflict with reality. Any actualization of the mind, individual or collective, produces aggression.

How and why did man's mind become the source of his aggression?

In order to understand the origin of man's aggression more clearly, I must go back to my definition of abstract thought. I repeat that the ancient Egyptians rightly placed the source of abstract thought in man's heart, and the ancient Romans *in pectore*, in the chest. In the New Testament (Luke) it is written: "Mary kept all these things, and pondered them in her heart." Abstract thought is, in fact, a wishful thought. Here we must ask ourselves again that important question: what inspires wishful thinking in man?

Man is an incomplete being. Being incomplete, man is vulnerable. In his variety of incomplete organs man always has one organ which is the most vulnerable, *locus minoris resistentiae*, which, when it breaks, kills life. This locus of least resistance, varies from man to man. An incomplete being is permanently aware of his most vulnerable spot. This spot dominates the rhythm of the entire life of an individual.

This vulnerable spot in man is the source of his wishful thinking. Somewhere in man's brain his weakest spot is registered. This registration in man's brain inspires and shapes abstract thoughts, ideals, ideologies, and political or religious attitudes.

How does this registration in man's brain of his locus of least resistance inspire and shape his abstract thoughts?

The only way a weak organ can: in the selfish way, the protective way. Man's abstract world of ideas is nothing but the protective shield for his weak spot, for his vulnerability, his chief weakness. This protective abstract world, being a wishful thought, is built to impress, thus creating an attitude of superiority, a superiority which leans on arrogance, the source of man's aggression. Whenever man's personal world is in contrast with the official ideologies, beliefs, or customs of society, he is in danger of facing breakdowns, depressions, or mental disorders.

The collective ideas of a gang, the source of the collective aggression, are of the same nature as the ideas of an individual; they are constructed around the weakest spot that the members of the gang have in common.

The mind's aggression could only have been discovered by an incomplete animal whose weakness and vulnerability meant more to him than the preservation of the species, and whose self-preservation, after the discovery of the mind, became a question of the mind.

Given the fact that abstract ideas have been constructed around the weakest biological spot, and given the fact that these spots vary from man to man, we have a variety of abstract protective ideas, a variety of ideologies, therefore a variety of aggressions in male humanity. This variety of aggression is evidence that the human male has no instinct of aggression; with an instinct of aggression there would be uniformity in the aggression.

When confronted by danger, man is a most unpredictable animal. With an instinct of aggression the behavior of an animal is predictable when in danger.

The main evidence that man has no instinct of aggression is that he has no innate technique of fighting. He has to learn how to fight or flee by imitating other animals. If he has not learned a technique to face it, man either panics or faints when confronted with danger, or enters into a state of stupor.

An animal has natural signals of aggression, which he displays when confronted with danger, trying to appear bigger and more impressive. A man shrinks when confronted by danger, trying to reduce his vulnerability. Man's signals of aggression and their display are his cultural achievements.

Another proof of man's lack of the instinct of aggression is that he has no naturally built-in safeguards to prevent him killing his own species. Any natural instinct of aggression is accompanied by a natural brake in killing its own species. Animals have "appeasement gestures," signals of submission which they respect. Men have no natural appeasement gestures, and even those agreed upon by signing international conventions are not respected by either the stronger or the weaker.

All scientists agree that the main object of the instinct of aggression in nature is the defense of the young. As far as the human species is concerned, this applies to woman but not to man. During air raids mothers protect their young while the men either panic or remain in an abulic or indecisive state. Darwin should have noticed that man has no instinctive aggression, or instincts for the preservation of the species, when he described in his notes of 4–7 September, 1833, how the Indians of Argentina, confronted by Spanish invaders, escaped in a panic "neglecting even their wives and children." Besides, throughout history, man has sent his sons to war to fight for an abstract idea.

Another instance showing that man's aggression is not part of his nature, but of his mind, is that an animal is never aggressive when safe and satiated, while man is often the reverse. The more satiated he feels, the more aggressive he becomes. His aggression can be influenced also by alcohol and drugs. Man is also the only animal who fights out of boredom.

Man can even turn aggression into a virtue. In some places it is a compliment to call someone aggressive.

The metaphysical origin of aggression can be deduced by its synonyms: militant, self-asserting, pushing, etc.; all products of individual or collective wishful thinking.

Man possesses another peculiarity created by his own mind: he is the only animal to gamble, to gamble his own and other people's lives. No other animal gambles; it is contrary to the logic of nature. Gambling is the attitude of an incomplete being who has nothing to lose and nothing to defend but his self-infatuation.

In the woodlands man separated from the apes because he was not aggressive. In the savannah man was in a state of neoteny, an exploratory phase guided by curiosity, which excluded aggression. If man had been aggressive in the savannah he could not have developed that exceptional increase of his brain.

Evidence that aggression stems from beliefs and self-infatuation is that there is no aggression in the mental illness known as "mania in circular psychosis," where the mind is incapable of fixing itself on a belief or of building something lasting around an idea.

Further proof that the source of man's aggression is in his mind is that aggression can be aroused by provoking the mind with propaganda, demagogy, suggestions, or hypnosis, or even with music. Psychological warfare plays an important part in any war. Primitive tribes who, being nearer to nature, therefore nearer to an instinct of aggression if it existed, need to perform war dances in order to acquire an aggressive spirit.

That man's aggression is in his mind can be determined by the fact that it can also be influenced positively or negatively by appropriate decorations or uniforms.

History offers evidence that the worst acts of aggression were acts of madness or folly. In his *Questions sur les miracles*, Voltaire stressed: *"La fureur de dominer est de toutes les maladies de l'esprit humain la plus terrible."*

Much aggression is caused by man's so-called "spirit of adventure." Man is the only adventurous animal, the only animal capable of being guided by illusions. An adventurous instinct would be contrary to the logic of nature.

The main instigator of aggression in history is the motto of human male beliefs: "Who is not with me is against me." This motto comes from the mind. It is the mind which established who is the enemy.

The worst type of aggression, such as wars and revolutions, are always fought for an idea or a belief.

Further evidence that aggression is dictated by man's abstract beliefs is that aggression increases with any change in beliefs.

The main sources of human aggression are racial, religious, and political prejudices. These are all created in the mind.

Jealousy, envy, moodiness, maliciousness, spitefulness, enmity, resentment, revengefulness are all states of mind, and are all sources of aggression.

Torture is another characteristic of the human species, and further evidence that aggression originates in the mind. Throughout history the torture of man by man has been committed in the name of an idea. Increase in the creativity of the human mind increased the perversion of torture, which is proved by the many torturers who possessed artistic minds.

Self-torture is another peculiarity of the human species, a product of the mind.

Major evidence that human aggression is a creation of man's mind, is the fact that it can be arrested or controlled by stronger aggression. Faced with admonishment, man changes his mind. Lenin was right when he said: "Terror is a method of persuasion."

The fact that aggression increases in societies where it pays to be aggressive, and vice-versa, is proof that it originates in man's mind, the mind of an opportunist.

Many writers insist that man was, and is, a hunter and a killer by nature because of his "killing imperative." In Spengler's *Man and Techniques*, we read the following: "The beast of prey is the highest form of active life. . . ." "The human race ranks highly because it belongs to the class of the beast of prey. . . ." "The life of a man is the life of a brave and splendid, cruel and cunning beast of prey. He lives by catching, killing, and consuming. Since he exists he must be master."

In Bertrand Russell's *Authority and the Individual* we read: "The old instincts that have come down to us from our tribal ancestors—all kinds of aggressive impulses inherited from generations of savages. . . ."

If man were a killer and hunter by nature he would never have become omnivorous.

If it is true that man is a beast of prey he would never have started agriculture or the domestication of animals.

The human species is the only species in nature to have mercenaries—professional killers. These killings are not dictated by any instinct of aggression but by calculated interest.

Depression, also, can induce aggressiveness and aggression. Depression is the state of mind of a pretentious adolescent whose conceit is far superior to his abilities. It is the state of mind of a narcissist in front of a crooked mirror.

Man considers a moral offense a reason for aggression. But man has no instinct of offense which triggers off the instinct of aggression. Offense stems from self-esteem. A Corsican kills his sister if he finds her in bed with a lover in her own native village, but he is able to live "with dignity" on her immoral earnings in Paris. In Sicily most killings are dictated by the idea of honor. Honor has nothing to do with instinct.

One source of human aggression is fairness, a sense of justice. But these are the human mind's creations and vary throughout peoples and history.

Many books have been written, trying to prove that one of the main sources of aggression is frustration, frustration caused by crowds.

What is frustration?

Frustration is nothing but self-infatuation in front of a mirror of reality. Man is frustrated in a crowd because his idea of himself is offended by reality. He is not frustrated, however, by being part of an even bigger crowd at a reception at Buckingham Palace or the White House. Man is frustrated when working in a crowded shop or factory, but seldom when he is dancing in an even more crowded night club. Man is never frustrated by the crowd that is applauding him, carrying him on their shoulders, or running after him in search of his autograph. He only hates crowds that do not flatter his self-infatuation. The human species is by nature a gregarious species.

Some people attribute the crime and aggression in big cities to overcrowding. But what about overcrowding in Moscow where often one room is shared by several people? This crowding does not breed crime and aggression. The people know that aggression will send them to the savannah of Siberia.

Some writers claim that density of population leads to increased aggression. Overpopulated areas such as Holland, Belgium, and Israel boast less crime than underpopulated areas such as Corsica or Sardinia.

In my view, humans are frustrated and irritated, therefore aggressive, if they think that they deserve a better position than that in which they find themselves. Essential conditions for this aggression is that someone else is in a better position. "Indigestion is never caused by what you eat, but by what other people eat." This old Spanish proverb describes a source of aggression in the human species.

Starting with J. J. Rousseau, many writers claim that civilization has increased aggression. But there is no connection between civilization and aggression. Civilization gave us the Rolls-Royce to travel in, but we were not prepared to accept it merely as an instrument of transport. The mind discovered that it was a status symbol which became the source of two aggressions, the aggression of those who owned it and the aggression of those who did not.

Any physical pain causes hurt and rage, therefore reaction. Any animal will react spontaneously to physical pain.

But what about man? Does physical pain trigger off his innate reaction?

Man's reaction to physical pain is dictated by his mind. Fanatics of ideas or beliefs will stand any amount of torture or pain.

"*Filling his world with statues, portraits and artificial creations of his mind, man has convinced himself that he is superior to nature.*"

"Imitation has no natural brakes in a being without an innate pattern of behavior."

"The ancient Greeks discovered the true source of aggression."

Man will even put up with pain without reacting, if his mind is satisfied that the pain is for his good, but he will not forgive a slight push if it destroys his self-infatuation. A man's reaction is far more aggressive if his beliefs are hurt rather than his skin.

That the source of man's aggression is in his mind can be determined by the following syllogistic reasoning: There is evidence that animals only kill their own species when they are forced to live in an unnatural environment.

There is also evidence that mankind kill each other.

This must mean then, that the human species lives in an unnatural environment. In fact the human species lives in a supernatural world, an abstract world governed by abstract thoughts.

Man populated his world with all manners of art in order to feel less isolated in the universe, and to embellish his abstract world. He has even gone so far in his self-infatuation as to prefer abstract beauties to natural ones.

Filling his world with statues, portraits, and artificial creations of his mind, man has convinced himself that he is superior to nature. It is in this conviction that we find another source of aggression. Art is the instigator of aggression.

Man also populated his world with pets. By reducing animals to his dependence, man was able to assume a feeling of importance, a man-made feeling. In nature there are no preferences, everything is equally important. The human search for importance is another source of aggression. Politicians must know this better than anyone. Their ultimate aim is to reduce the people to being their pets.

Perversion, too, is a source of aggression.

What is perversion and why is it peculiar to humans? Perversion is excess.

What creature can reach excess? Only an incomplete being in search of completion.

In what activities can excess occur? Excess can only occur in imitation, the activity of a being whose aim is to be like another. With Homo sapiens, with the development of the mind and its imagination, the step from being the same, to being better than other beings was short. Man forced the imitation beyond the imitated. This brought him to perversion. Imitation has no natural brakes in a being without an innate pattern of behavior.

MAN: THE FALLEN APE

The ancient Greeks discovered the true source of aggression. They describe it in their myth of the birth of Athena, their goddess of war. "Zeus himself," explained Hesiod in his *The Theogony*, "gave birth from his own head to owl-eyed Tritogeneia, the awful, the strife-stirring, the host-leader . . . who delights in tumults and wars and battles." . . . "The master of craft Zeus alone bore her out of his holy head," explained Homer in one of his hymns. In Pindar's verses we see the consequence to the harmony of the cosmos, caused by her birth, in the following lines: "At the stroke of the bronze-heeled axe Athena sprung from the height of her father's head with a strong cry. The sky shivered before her and earth our mother too."

In Homer's *Iliad* we see how the idea of war came only from the head of Zeus. "The Sir of gods and men . . . said to Athena, 'go at once into the Trojan and Achaean hosts, and contrive that the Trojans shall be the first to break their oaths and set upon the Achaeans.' This was what Athena was already eager to do, so down she darted from the topmost summits of Olympus."

Plato in his *Cratylus* said that Athena is "mind and thought."

In Homer's "Hymn to Aphrodite," the power of Athena is evident. "All creatures in heaven and on earth pay homage to Aphrodite, but with Athena her power disappears."

In Aeschylus' *Eumenides* we read Athena's own words: "No mother bore me, in all things my heart turns to the male, save only for wedlock, and I incline wholly to the father." Athena, the goddess of men's aggression, is therefore the daughter of a father. She had no mother.

The Jews, too, knew the real source of aggression.

"The Lord is a man of war," we read in Exodus.

Who is the Lord?

"Thou shalt not kill," the Lord commanded, this omnipotent Lord who was a creation of the human mind, and therefore knew the human mind. Would the Lord have commanded humans not to kill if it was in their instinct? He knew that the source of killing was in people's minds, and He knew that He could manipulate the human mind. To give evidence of His power, He ordered Abraham to kill his son Isaac for His sake. By his behavior Abraham not only showed that killing is dictated by the mind, but that the mind and its abstract beliefs are superior to any instinct, including the instinct to preserve the species.

Laughter

In the opinion of scientists, man is the only animal in nature capable of laughter. What no one has pointed out is that man is also the only laughable being in nature. Other animals, human children and human females, are only laughable when imitating men.

Aggression and laughter were born at the same time and in the same place: in man's mind. Whenever a self-infatuated person descends from his abstract world into reality, a laughable situation occurs.

When man entered the savannah he was a frightened being. With the discovery of his mind and on its heels the adoption of aggression, the fear increased. Laughter is the sudden relaxation of a perpetually frightened being: it is caused by a decrease in the fear induced by the presence of someone bereft of his self-infatuation, and therefore shaken in the source of his aggression.

Bergson's *du mécanique plaqué sur du vivant*, which Chaplin exploited, means man lowered from his "dignity," his self-infatuation, his arrogance.

In my view, laughter is a temporary freedom from genuine or anticipated aggression. Hysterical laughter after an escaped peril demonstrates its true meaning. It is a relief.

People who laugh at anything are those afraid that their vulnerability will be exposed. This laughter is a self-defense. Highly vulnerable people develop an aprioristic laughter; they laugh for no reason, hoping to prevent aggression.

Unfortunate or tragic news can trigger off nervous laughter. It is caused by the lifting of an anticipatory obsession—relief from a dread of what might have happened. It is the end of a period of apprehension.

Smiling is another peculiarity of the human species.

What inspired humans to smile?

Like laughter, smiles can also be dictated by cultural inheritance, education or social convenience. They have also become signs of displays of superiority. This distracts writers from their true origin and meaning.

In my view, a natural smile is inspired by the scar left on the brain by the primordial expression on the human face in the woodlands, an expression of happiness, security, and innocence.

Man's face today is the face of the savannah, a face of fear and anxiety. To this face of fear and anxiety, Homo sapiens added the fear of aggression. Man's face only reverts to its primordial expression when displaying innocent smiles. The closest approximation to these innocent smiles occur on the human face when it is confronted with natural beauty.

What is beauty?

Beauty is whatever relaxes us, whatever gives us peace of mind, whatever, by external signs, can indicate that it is not aggressive.

Why then do humans only seldom enjoy beauty?

By assisting liberation from fear, beauty provokes the desire to possess it, to own it. This leads to aggression. Men, in wanting to possess or own beauty in order to have lasting protection from it, end up in protecting beauty. Possession of beauty always opens the way to envy and jealousy.

In our unstable, materialistic world, where money is a sign of power, humans have come to the following position: beauty has become whatever is valuable in monetary terms because it gives an illusion of protection and security, an illusion because in reality it creates anxiety.

Sexual and Natural Selection

Many scientists glorify man's aggression because it is beneficial to "sexual selection."

"Hence it is the males that fight together and sedulously display their charm before the female; and the victors transmit their superiority to their male off-spring," Darwin explains in *The Descent of Man*. Darwin can be excused for having picked a special moment in British history, in a particular social, economic and intellectual atmosphere, as the universal law for the human species. Darwin never witnessed the consequences of free medicine and social legislation, which help what he calls the "less fit" to survive and reproduce more than the "fit." One cannot, however, excuse modern Darwinists who persist in acclaiming "sexual selection," when there are obvious examples that it is not the "fittest" who have the better chance of survival and reproduction in a Welfare State.

Darwin and Darwinists have never defined the meaning of the "fittest"; possibly because there is no such thing as the "fittest" in the human species, a species with no natural specialization.

"That the males of all mammalians eagerly pursue the female is notorious to everyone," Darwin writes in *The Descent of Man*. "Males of mammalians pursue the females."

Humans are mammals, *ergo* human males pursue human females. This is a pure syllogism, far from the truth, particularly nowadays, with the emancipation of woman.

The human species became a unique species because of the lack of any aggressive instinct in the human male. Without the instinct of aggression there can be no natural or "sexual" selection. Many authors wrongly confuse "sexual selection" with jealousy,

MAN: THE FALLEN APE

"machismo," exhibitionism, or social rivalry, which are states of mind.

In the world of mammals sexual selection decides the fittest male. The female automatically agrees to be inseminated by the fittest male. With the human species, this makes no sense.

A fit and successful man in a military, academic, or business career, is not necessarily sexually fit. Professional success needs concentration, which saps sexual performance.

Besides, we can presume that a successful man transmits his qualities to his son. Would the same qualities, however, be successful with the new generation, bearing in mind the changing values of the times?

But even if men are successful in certain fields in the eyes of other men, it does not mean that women agree. Many men admired Napoleon, but few women.

Darwin forgot that while women may be charmed by genius or physical beauty, they marry and procreate with what Kierkegaard called "the fat, self-indulgent mediocrity."

Sexual maniacs or frustrated "Latin lovers" have more chance of procreating than conscientious, good-looking Swedes. And what about sexual caprices? Karl Marx married a German aristocrat but he had a child with her maid.

The human species is the least likely species to maintain the validity of "sexual selection." Most humans were conceived, either in a drunken or drugged state, or in wedlock. "Sexual selection," even if it existed in man's nature, could never operate inside the institution of marriage. Ever since the adolescent revolution, sexual relationships have been regulated by religious, social, moral, and economic rules, which preclude natural and sexual selection.

Natural and sexual selection cannot exist in a species in which sick people can procreate and transmit their illnesses to their progeny. Natural and sexual selection cannot exist in a species which buys sex, or punishes adultery, or uses synthetic hormones.

That fashion, publicity, and films can dictate sex appeal is evidence that there is no innate criterion for sexual selection in the human species. Today, actors and actresses inspire the sexual taste. In ancient Rome they were considered second-rate people.

Above all, we must stress that the more responsible, and the healthier morally and physically, the couples are, the fewer children they have compared with couples with the opposite characteristics.

We have seen that human procreation is the result of three obsessions: the pleasure of sex, the pleasure of the mind, and the search for immortality. These, being obsessions, cannot produce selective breeding.

Being a singular species, humanity has produced a phenomenon: vast numbers of homosexuals. They are often a fit and very successful element in the struggle for existence but they seldom reproduce. The Catholic Church was and still is dominated by asexuals. What is more, this hierarchy of asexuals has established the pattern of sexual behavior for millions of people for centuries.

In order to discuss "natural selection" we need a criterion for it. As humans have no natural specialization, we can only have an abstract criterion of "natural selection."

"From the remotest times successful tribes have supplanted other tribes," Darwin wrote in *The Descent of Man*. He did not, however, define "successful tribes." Babylon was occupied by Assyrians, Crete by Greeks, ancient Rome by Vandals, Byzantium by Turks, Renaissance Rome by Spaniards and Paris by Prussians. In each case the occupied were more advanced in culture and civilization than the occupiers. We have also seen, throughout history, larger countries taking over smaller countries, regardless of whether the smaller countries were more advanced from a natural point of view.

"Do not obtain your slaves from Britons, for they are so stupid and dull that they are not fit for slaves," Cicero advised. Eighteen centuries later, a short time for any "natural selection" to succeed so radically, Britons became the most "successful tribe" in the world.

Natural selection cannot succeed in a species where lunatics can kill Presidents with man-made weapons, or where Presidents may be lunatics.

What kind of natural selection could exist in a dictatorship? "The less favored individuals will tend to die out," Darwinists say. This may be true, but it is the "less favored" by the official policy who are dying out, those who are usually more favored by nature. In Nazi Germany, the Jews, the "less favored" by the

Nazi policy, indeed, died out, but this did not mean that they were "less favored" from a natural or cultural point of view.

Unnatural Selection

With the discovery of the mind, man underwent massive change. Instead of pursuing his own evolution, as he had done in the past, he started adapting the environment to his body and mind. Man's capacity for exploiting natural resources convinced him that he had reached perfection. He arrived at a state of self-infatuation that continues to this day.

The disturbing gap between mind and body increased. The consequences of this were: psychosomatic disorder, psychosis, neurosis (troubles unknown in the sub-human world), and increased apprehension and fear of pain, vulnerability, and death.

The result of man's self-infatuation has been also a progressive destruction of his own environment. Until recently, man has had an illusion that natural resources were inexhaustible. We realize now that much of the so-called progress of the present generation is at the expense of future generations.

Our ideas of progress and perfection can be explained by the uniqueness of our species. In the sub-human world the individual serves the species; the present generations living, and often sacrificing, for the future. In the human world, there is an *après moi le déluge* attitude—in men by conviction, in women by imitation of men.

An unnatural environment, the creation of man's mind, has produced an unnatural selection in our species. This unnatural selection generates unfit individuals.

"Man is the first species that can influence its further evolution. By therapeutic agents and techniques, he can ensure the survival of the less-than-fittest, and so frustrate the evolutionary process. After considering the moral and spiritual, as well as physical factors, this may be what he wishes to do. But it is essential that those involved in health care, political as well as medical, face the problem. At the moment it is not being faced at all," stressed Professor Paul Turner at the British Royal Society Congress of 1975.

The increase in population increases the number of the unfit. In any community this weak and vulnerable element, being more and more numerous, sooner or later, succeeds in imposing its ideology on the rest of the community. Political ideologies and economic policies, catering to the needs of the least fit, will one day create a gap between productivity and human needs, and that gap will be so large that the race could be annihilated—by famine, by epidemic, or by an unpredictable biological catastrophe.

The improvements in medicine and in social services, particularly since the beginning of this century, have accelerated the increase in world population. The world population, calculated at approximately 250 million at the end of the Roman Empire, had doubled by the middle of the seventeenth century. It took two centuries to double again, reaching one billion around 1850. Only a hundred years later the world population passed three billion. Now, the world population doubles every thirty-five years. *Rebus sic statibus*, without any further improvement in medicine or social services, in three hundred years we will have around 1,790 billion, and in five hundred years, around 114,680 billion people occupying an earth's surface of 54,469,928 square miles.

The population increase is due not only to the increase in the number of the unfit, but also to the increase of the young and the old. The rate of increase of the young and old can be deduced by the following: in 1800, in advanced countries, out of each 1,000 live births, 480 reached the age of 20, and 210 reached that of 60. The figures for 1950, respectively, were 920 and 650.

We see, therefore, that an increase in population is mainly an increase in the number of the economically unproductive groups. The increasing size and need of the economically unproductive— the unfit, the old and the young—are an increasing burden to the economically productive.

With every day that passes these groups are growing farther and farther apart, each group having its own ideas, its own values, and often its own language. The factions within the social structure of the modern world are creating ever greater tension and strain.

"A sort of militant hysteria threatens our species, [and the hysteria] may lead us down, step by step, to a cruel and degenerate belligerence to a life which will have few interest beyond pain, hate and elementary lust, and few virtues except a Spartan endurance," wrote H. G. Wells before World War II, in his book *A Short History of the World*. The "militant hysteria" is clear evidence of the failure of man's mind to find a pattern of life which is in his interest and in that of his species.

Russian Nobel Prize winner Andrei Sakharov explained even more clearly that man has failed to find a solution for the life of his species: "Civilization is imperiled by a universal thermonuclear war, a catastrophic hunger for most of mankind. . . . a spreading of mass myths that put entire peoples and continents under the power of cruel and treacherous demagogues, and destruction from the unforeseeable consequences of swift changes in the conditions of life on our planet."

Can it be that man's last chance is, once again, woman?

Can the human female, who once saved the fallen ape in the savannah now save god-man, fallen with the omnipotence of his mind? Can she save him from the new savannah in which he finds himself now, more frightened than ever before, frightened by his most dangerous enemy, himself? Is her instinct for the preservation of the species strong enough to prevent this catastrophe?

History, alas, shows that woman's instinct for adaptation is stronger than her instinct for the preservation of the species.

When the adolescent male rebelled by taking the dominating role and inventing abstract ideas and beliefs, woman adapted herself to the absurd world man had created. Proof of woman's instinct of adaptation being stronger than her instinct for the preservation of the species lies in the fact that never in the history of mankind have we seen women rebelling against their husbands' decisions to send their children off to war, to be killed for an abstract belief.

We are now witnessing a sad spectacle. Around the world, men, who have no instinct for the preservation of the species, are discussing birth control in abstract terms. Women, who do possess this instinct and should, therefore, be entitled to deal with this problem, are not rebelling against this. Their instinct of adaptation is stronger than their instinct for the preservation of the species.

What is even more tragic for the human species is that defects in woman's instinct of adaptation do not favor her instinct for the preservation of the species. On the contrary, when woman recognizes defects in her instinct of adaptation, she starts to imitate man. She tries to be equal to man. She starts to defend her vulnerability by adopting the abstract beliefs or ideologies invented by man to protect his defects. She even goes so far as to imitate another of man's attitudes, for she uses arrogance and aggression to defend her adopted ideologies. Being imitations, these postures are often more extreme than those in man.

By imitating man, woman has also succeeded in imitating one of man's most harmful vices. Note these passages from a report of January 1976, on "Female alcoholics" in England: "There are many indications that the number of women alcoholics becoming apparent, or presenting for help, has increased since the first report. Thirteen years ago, with the first figures from alcoholism information centres, it was apparent that the incidence was 1 female for every 7 or 8 male alcoholics; three years ago the ratio had dropped to 1 female for every 4 or 5 males; and the latest figures would indicate that in some areas the ratio is now 3 males to 1 female. But it should be emphasised that these are the figures for those presenting themselves at information centres for help: there must be a vast number of female alcoholics, perhaps drinking quietly at home during the day, who have not so far become apparent. . . . Some of the women were found to have a 'spiteful' attitude towards their drinking husbands, stating they felt that what was good for their husbands was good for them. . . ."

One can only hope that women will return to reality and induce man to listen to her natural wisdom. She can do this by ceasing to strive for equality with man. Equality with man means descending to man's pathetic and ridiculous level. Woman should liberate herself from imitating man and from adapting to man's abstract world.

Woman's common sense is part of a woman's nature and that nature only comes to light when she is not imitating man or adapting herself to his world. To have the courage and the

MAN: THE FALLEN APE

chance to use her common sense, woman needs economic independence. Woman could, perhaps, ensure this independence by inheriting wealth and by insisting on a state maintenance in Communist countries. With woman's economic independence, man will be forced to come down from his abstract pedestal, and start living life instead of inventing it, acting it, or philosophizing about it.

Women collectively should seek important constitutional changes. It would be more in harmony with the nature of the human species if legislative and judicial powers were in women's hands, and the executive power in men's. Any woman with her first child becomes a natural legislator and a natural judge. For men, law and justice are creations of an abstract mind.

Man, after all, has no innate sense of organization. Man's organizations are either inspired by some transcendental considerations, or they are a cultural inheritance of abstract ideas of the past. An organization, by its very nature, is concerned with reality, a changing reality, a future. Organizations, inspired by abstract thoughts, and especially by those belonging to the past, are, therefore, far from being realistic.

An honest and unbiased analysis of history shows that societies whose organizations were inspired and influenced by women have succeeded in creating harmony among the different groups of their populations, and in realizing, through co-operation, conditions of high economic productivity, both factors of essential importance for a species which generates an increasing number of unfit and unproductive individuals.

Bibliography

Adkins, A. W. H., *Moral Values and Political Behaviour in Ancient Greece*. London: Chatto & Windus, 1972.

Adler, A., *Studie Über Minderwertigkeit von Organen*. Wien, 1972.

Alexander, S., *Beauty and Other Forms of Value*. London: Macmillan, 1933.

Arambourgh, C., *La Genèse de l'Humanité*. Paris: P.U.F., 1969.

Ardrey, R., *African Genesis*. London: Collins, 1961.

———, *The Territorial Imperative*. London: Collins, 1967.

———, *The Social Contract*. London: Collins, 1970.

Arnold, E. V., *Roman Stoicism*. Cambridge University Press, 1911.

Bauthoul, G., *Les Mentalités*. Paris: P.U.F., 1961.

Bayard, J. P., *Histoire des Légendes*. Paris: P.U.F., 1961.

Bayer, R., *Essais sur la Méthode en Esthétique*. Paris: Flammarion, 1953.

Beach, F. A., and Ford, C. S., *Pattern of Sexual Behaviour*. New York: Harper & Row, 1951.

Beauvoir, Simone de, *The Second Sex*. Paris: Knopf, 1953.

Beer De, G. R., *Embryos and Ancestors*. London: Chapman & Hall, 1953.

Behn, F., *L'Art Préhistorique en Europe*. Paris: P.B.P., 1970.

Berelson, B., and Steiner, G. A., *Human Behaviour*. New York: Harcourt, Brace & World, 1964.

Berne, E., *Games People Play*. Harmondsworth, Penguin, 1969.

Blanc, A. C., "Some Evidence for the Ideologies of Early Man," in *Social Life of Early Man*. S. L. Washburn, ed., Chicago: Aldine, 1961.

Bloch, H. A., and Niederhoffer, A., *The Gang: A Study in Adolescent Behavior*. New York: Philosophical Library, 1958.

Bloch, R., *The Origins of Rome*. London: Thames & Hudson, 1960.

Bokun, B., *The Pornocracy*. London: Stacey, 1971.

———, *Spy in the Vatican*. New York: Praeger, 1973.

Bokun, P., *Pshiha I Tjielo*. Split, 1974.

Bolton, N., *The Psychology of Thinking*. London: Methuen, 1972.

Bronowski, J., *The Ascent of Man*. London: BBC Publishers, 1973.

Bulfinch, T., *The Age of Fable*. New York: Mentor, 1962.

Buraud, G., *Les Masques*. Paris: Le Sueil, 1948.

Burckhardt, J., *History of Greek Culture*. London: Constable, 1963.

Burn, A. R., *The Pelican History of Greece*. London: Penguin, 1971.

Burton, M., *Infancy in Animals*. London: Hutchinson, 1956.

Buytendijk, F. J. J., *L'Homme et l'Animal*. Paris: Gallimard, 1965.

Calder, N., *The Mind of Man*. London: BBC Publications, 1970.

Campbell, B. G., *Human Evolution: An Introduction to Man's Adaption*. Chicago: Aldine, 1965.

Campbell, J., ed., *Myth, Religion, and the Mother Right: Selected Writings of J. J. Bachofen*. Princeton: University Press, 1967.

Cannon, W. B., *Bodily Changes in Pain, Hunger, Fear and Rage*. New York: Appleton-Century, 1964.

Carritt, E. F., *The Theory of Beauty*. London: Methuen, 1914.

———, *La Maîtrise du Comportement*. Paris: P.U.F., 1956.

Chauchard, P., *Physiologie des Moeurs*. Paris: P.U.F., 1961.

Chauvin, R., *Les Sociétés Animales*. Paris: Plon, 1963.

Chiaramonte, N., *The Paradox of History*. London: Weidenfeld and Nicolson, 1970.

Childe, V. G., *The Dawn of European Civilization*. London: Routledge and K. Paul, 1925.

Cipolla, C. M., ed., *The Economic Decline of Empires*. London: Methuen, 1970.

Clairborne, R., *Climate, Man and History*. London: Angus & Robertson, 1970.

Clark, G., *World Prehistory*. Cambridge: University Press, 1961.

———, *Prehistoric Societies*. London: Hutchinson, 1965.

Cohen, A., *Two-Dimensional Man*. London: Routledge and K. Paul, 1974.

Colbert, E. H., *Evolution of the Vertebrates*. New York: Wiley, 1955.

Cole, Sonia, *The Prehistory of Southern Africa*. London: Weidenfeld and Nicolson, 1964.

———, *The Neolithic Revolution*. London: British Museum, 1970.

Coon, C. S., *The Living Races of Man*. London: J. Cape, 1966.

———, *The History of Man*. London: Penguin, 1967.

Crow, W. B., *A History of Magic, Witchcraft, and Occultism*. London: Abacus, 1968.

Darlington, C. D., *Evolution of Genetic Systems*. London: Olivier and Boyd, 1932.

Darwin, F., *The Life and Letters of Charles Darwin*. London: J. Murray, 1887.

Dastre, A., *La Vie et la Mort*. Paris: Flammarion, 1908.

de Bono, E., *The Mechanism of the Mind*. London: J. Cape, 1969.

de Burgh, W. G., *The Legacy of the Ancient World*. London: Penguin, 1953.

DeRopp, R. S., *Sex Energy*. New York: Delacorte Press, 1969.

Deutsche, Helene, *The Psychology of Women*. New York: Coward-McCann, 1948.

DeVore, J., ed., *Primate Behavior*. New York: Holt, Rinehart and Winston, 1965.

Dobzhansky, T., *Mankind Evolving*. New Haven: Yale University Press, 1962.

Dodds, E. R., *The Greeks and the Irrational*. Berkeley: University of California Press, 1968.

Drever, J., *A Dictionary of Psychology*. Harmondsworth, England: Penguin, 1952.

Drucker, H. M., *The Political Uses of Ideology*. London: Macmillan, 1974.

Dunne, J., *City of the Gods*. London: Sheldon Press, 1974.

Edelstein, L., *The Meaning of Stoicism*. Cambridge, Mass.: Harvard University Press, 1966.

Eibl-Eibesfeldt, I., *Ethology: the Biology of Behavior*. New York: Holt, Rinehart and Winston, 1970.

———, *Love and Hate*. London: Methuen, 1973.

Eimerl, S., and de Vore, I., *The Primates*. London: Time-Life International, 1967.

Emery, W. B., *Archaic Egypt*. London: Penguin, 1961.

Engels, F., *Dijalektika Prirode*. Zagreb: Kultura, 1950.

Escarpit, R., *L'Humour*. Paris: P.U.F., 1960.

Evans-Pritchard, E. E., *Theories of Primitive Religions*. Oxford University Press, 1965.

Eysenck, H. J., *Fact and Fiction in Psychology*. London: Penguin, 1965.

Fletcher, R., *Instinct in Man*. New York: International University Press, 1968.

Flores, C., *La Memoire*. Paris: P.U.F., 1974.

Foos, B. M., ed., *Determinants of Infant Behavior*. London: Methuen, 1961.

Frazer, J. G., *The Golden Bough*. London: Macmillan, 1922.

Freedman, J. L., *Crowding and Behavior*. San Francisco: W. H. Freeman, 1975.

Freud, S., *Moses and Monotheism*. London: Hogarth Press, 1974.

Friedan, B., *The Feminine Mystique*. New York: W. W. Norton, 1963.

Fromm, E., *The Sane Society*. London: Routledge and K. Paul, 1963.

———, *The Anatomy of Human Destructiveness*. London: J. Cape, 1974.

Gaillois, R., *Les Jeux et les Hommes*. Paris: 1958.

Gibson, A. B., *Muse and Thinker*. London: Penguin, 1972.

Gilbert, J., *Myths and Legends of Ancient Rome*. Hamlyn, 1970.

Gimbutas, M., *The Gods and Goddesses of Old Europe*. London: Thames & Hudson, 1974.

Glaser, I., *Opca Psihopatologija*. Zagreb: Skolska Knjiga, 1958.

Grant, M., *Myths of the Greeks and Romans*. New York: Mentor, 1962.

———, *Myth of the Greek Heroes*. London: Penguin, 1973.

Graves, R., *The Greek Myths*. London: Penguin, 1973.

Green, R., *Tales of Ancient Egypt*. London: Penguin, 1970.

———, *Myths of the Norsemen*. London: Penguin, 1972.

Gregg, V., *Human Memory*. London: Methuen, 1975.

Gruber, H. E., *Darwin on Man*. London: Wildwood House, 1974.

Guilford, J. P., *The Nature of Human Intelligence*. New York: McGraw-Hill, 1967.

Hadfield, J. A., *Childhood and Adolescence*. London: Penguin, 1962.

Haim, A., *Adolescent Suicide*. London: Tavistock, 1974.

Haldane, J. B. S., *The Causes of Evolution*. London: Longmans, 1974.

Hass, H., *The Human Animal*. London: Corgi Books, 1932.

Hawkes, J., *Prehistory*. London: Allen & Unwin, 1963.

———, *The First Great Civilizations*. London: Hutchinson, 1973.

Heidel, A., *The Babylonian Genesis*. Chicago: University of Chicago Press, 1942.

Huisman, D., *L'Esthétique*. Paris: P.U.F., 1961.

Huizinga, J., *Homo Ludens: A Study of the Play Element in Culture*. London: Routledge and K. Paul, 1949.

Hutchinson, R. W., *Prehistoric Crete*. London: Penguin, 1962.

Huxley, A., *Ape and Essence*. New York: Harper & Bros., 1948.

Huxley, J., *Evolution: A Modern Synthesis*. London: Allen & Unwin, 1963.

———, *Essays of a Humanist*. New York: Harper & Row, 1964.

Jaccard, P., *Histoire Sociale du Travail*. Paris: Payot, 1960.

Jung, C. G., *Four Archetypes*. London: Routledge and K. Paul, 1972.

———, *Psychology of the Unconscious*. London: K. Paul, 1919.

Kenny, A. J. P., Longuet-Higgins, H. C., and Waddington, C. H., *Nature of Mind*. Edinburgh: University Press.

Kiefer, O., *Sexual Life in Ancient Rome*. London: Panther, 1969.

Kinsey, A. C., Pomeroy, W. B., Martin, C. E., *Sexual Behavior in the Human Male*. Philadelphia: Saunders, 1948.

———, *Sexual Behavior in the Human Female*. Philadelphia: Saunders, 1948.

Kintsch, W., *Learning Memory and Conceptual Processes*. New York: Academic Press, 1970.

Kjellberg, E., and Säflund, G., *Greek and Roman Art 3000 B.C. to 500 A.D.* London: Faber and Faber, 1968.

Koffka, K., *The Growth of the Mind*. London: K. Paul., 1946.

Kuhn, T. S., *La Structure des Révolutions Scientifiques*. Paris: Flammarion, 1972.

Lantier, R., *La Vie Préhistorique*. Paris: P.U.F., 1970.

Laufer, M., *Adolescent Disturbance and Breakdown*. Harmondsworth: Penguin, 1975.

Lausch, E., *Manipulation—Is Your Brain Your Own?* London: Fontana, 1975.

Lawick-Goodall, Jane van, *In the Shadow of Man*. London: Collins, 1971.

Leakey, L. S. B., *Olduvai Gorge 1951–1961*. Cambridge: University Press, 1965.

Le Cros Clark, W. E., *History of Primates*. London: British Museum, 1949.

———, and Leakey, L. S. B., *Miocene Hominoidea of East Africa*. London: British Museum, 1951.

———, *The Antecedents of Man*. Edinburgh: University Press, 1971.

Lederer, W., *The Fear of Women*. New York: Harcourt, Brace, Jovanovich, 1968.

Lévi-Strauss, C., *Anthropologie Structurale*. Paris: Plon, 1958.

———, *La Pensée Sauvage*. Paris: Plon, 1962.

———, *Mythologiques*. Paris: Plon, 1967.

Lewis, J., *The Uniqueness of Man*. London: Lawrence & Wishart, 1974.

Littman, R., *The Greek Experiment*. London: Thames and Hudson, 1974.

Lorenz, K., *King Solomon's Ring*. London: Methuen, 1952.

———, *Man Meets Dog*. London: Methuen, 1954.

———, *On Aggression*. London: Methuen, 1972.

———, *Les Huits Péchés Capitaux de Notre Civilization*. Paris: Flammarion, 1973.

———, *Evolution et Modification du Comportement*. Paris: P.B.P., 1974.

Lund, E., Pihl, M. and Sløk, J., *A History of European Ideas.* London: Hurst & Co., 1971.

Luria, A. R., *The Working Brain.* London: Penguin, 1973.

Malinowski, B., *The Sexual Life of Savages.* London: Routledge and K. Paul, 1964.

Marler, P., and Hamilton, W. J., *Mechanism of Animal Behavior.* New York: Wiley, 1966.

Masters, W. H., and Johnson, V. E., *Human Sexual Response.* Boston: Little, Brown, 1966.

Mates, B., *Stoic Logic.* Berkeley: University of California Press, 1953.

Maynard, Smith, J., *The Theory of Evolution.* London: Penguin, 1958.

McGurk, H., *Growing and Changing.* London: Methuen, 1975.

Mendel, G., *Anthropologie Deférentielle.* Paris: P.B.P., 1972.

Metalnikov, S., *La Lutte Contre la Mort.* Paris: Gallimard, 1937.

Meyer, F., *Problématique de l'Évolution.* Paris: P.U.F., 1954.

Milgram, S., *Obedience to Authority.* London: Tavistock, 1974.

Millar, S., *The Psychology of Play.* London: Penguin, 1968.

Miller, N. E., and Dollard, J., *Social Learning and Imitation.* London: K. Paul, 1941.

Milton, J. P., *Prophecy Interpreted.* London: Chapman, 1974.

Monod, J., *Le Hasard et la Nécessité.* Paris: Ed. du Seuil, 1970.

Montagu, A., *On Being Human.* New York: Hawthorn Books, 1967.

———, *The Natural Superiority of Women.* New York: Macmillan, 1968.

———, ed., *Man and Aggression.* Oxford: University Press, 1973.

Morgan, E., *The Descent of Woman.* London: Souvenir Press, 1972.

Morris, D., *The Naked Ape.* London: J. Cape, 1967.

———, *The Human Zoo.* London: Corgi Books, 1971.

———, *Intimate Behavior.* London: Corgi Books, 1972.

Mumford, L., *Technique et Civilisation.* Paris: Ed. du Seuil., 1951.

Musgrove, F., *Youth and the Social Order.* London: Routledge and K. Paul, 1964.

Napier, J., and Napier, P., *Primate Biology*. London: Academie Press, 1970.

Napier, P., *Monkeys and Apes*. London: Hamlyn, 1970.

Oakley, K. P., *Man the Toolmaker*. London: British Museum, 1961.

Oraison, M., *Le Mystère Humain de la Sexualité*. Paris: Ed. du Seuil., 1966.

Orgel, L. E., *The Origins of Life*. London: Chapman and Hall, 1953.

Otto, W., *The Homeric Gods*. London: Thames & Hudson, 1954.

Paffard, M., *Inglorious Wordsworths: A Study of Some Transcendental Experiences in Childhood and Adolescence*. London: Hodder & Stoughton, 1973.

Parker, A., *States of Mind: ESP and Altered States of Consciousness*. London: Malaby Press, 1975.

Parrot, A., *Sumerian Art*. Fontana UNESCO Art Books, 1970.

Pavlov, I. P., *Conditioned Reflexes*. London: Clarendon Press, 1927.

Pfeiffer, J. E., *The Emergence of Man*. London: Thomas Nelson & Sons, 1970.

Penfield, W., *The Mystery of the Mind*. Princeton: Princeton University Press, 1975.

Perowne, S., *The End of the Roman World*. London: Hodder & Stoughton, 1966.

———, *Roman Mythology*. London: Hamlyn, 1969.

Phillips, J. L., *The Origins of Intellect: Piaget's Theory*. San Francisco: W. H. Freeman, 1969.

Piaget, J., *Judgment and Reasoning in the Child*. London: Routledge, 1951.

———, *Play Dreams and Imitation in Childhood*. London: Routledge, 1951.

———, *Origin of Intelligence in the Child*. London: Routledge, 1953.

Piggott, S., ed., *The Fall of Civilisation*. London: Thames & Hudson, 1961.

Pilbeam, D., *The Evolution of Man*. London: Thames & Hudson, 1970.

Plamenatz, J., *Democracy and Illusion*. London: Longman, 1973.

Poems of Heaven and Hell from Ancient Mesopotamia. London: Penguin, 1971.

Poroda, E., *L'Art dans le Monde*. Paris: Albin Michel, 1962.

Pribram, K. H., ed., *Adaption*. Harmondsworth: Penguin, 1969.

———, *Mood, States and Mind*. Harmondsworth: Penguin, 1969.

Radin, P., *La Religion Primitive*. Paris: Gallimard, 1941.

Read, C., *The Origin of Man*. Cambridge: University Press, 1925.

Richardson, A., *Mental Imagery*. London: Routledge and K. Paul, 1969.

Rist, J. M., *Stoic Philosophy*. Cambridge: University Press, 1969.

Rochlin, G., *Man's Aggression*. London: Constable, 1973.

Roe, D., *Prehistory*. London: Macmillan, 1970.

Romer, A. S., *Man and the Vertebrates*. London: Penguin, 1954.

Rostand, J., *La Biologie et l'Avenir Humain*. Paris: A. Michel, 1950.

Rostovtzeff, W., *The Social and Economic History of the Roman Empire*. Oxford: Clarendon Press, 1926.

———, *A History of the Ancient World*. Oxford: Clarendon Press, 1927.

Russell, C., and Russell, W. M. C., *Human Behavior*. London: A. Deutsch, 1961.

Sakharov, A. D., *Progress, Coexistence, and Intellectual Freedom*. Harmondsworth: Penguin, 1969.

Samburski, S., *Physics of the Stoics*. London: Routledge and K. Paul, 1959.

Sanbach, F. H., *The Stoics*. London: Chatto & Windus, 1975.

Sandstrom, C. I., *The Psychology of Childhood and Adolescence*. London: Penguin, 1968.

Schafer, E., *The Divine Woman*. Berkeley: University of California Press, 1973.

Schaller, G. B., *The Mountain Gorilla*. Chicago: University Press, 1963.

Scholem, G., *The Messianic Idea in Judaism*. London: Allen & Unwin, 1971.

Scott, J. P., *Aggression*. Chicago: University Press, 1958.

Sherwin-White, A. N., *Racial Prejudice in Imperial Rome*. Cambridge: University Press, 1967.

Simpson, G. G., *The Meaning of Evolution*. New Haven: Yale University Press, 1951.

Skinner, B. F., *Science and Human Behavior*. New York: Macmillan, 1953.

——, *Beyond Freedom and Dignity*. New York: Alfred A. Knopf, 1971.

——, *About Behaviorism*. London: J. Cape, 1974.

Smart, N., *The Religious Experience of Mankind*. London: Fontana, 1971.

Smith, J. M., *The Theory of Evolution*. London: Penguin, 1972.

Spilsbury, R., *Providence Lost—A Critic of Darwinism*. Oxford: University Press, 1974.

Stenhouse, D., *The Evolution of Intelligence*. London: Allen & Unwin, 1973.

Stobart, J. C., *The Grandeur That Was Rome*. London: Sidgwick & Jackson, 1912.

Storr, A., *Human Aggression*. London: Penguin, 1972.

——, *The Dynamics of Creation*. London: Secker & Warburg, 1972.

Szasz, T., *Ideology and Insanity*. London: Calder and Boyards, 1973.

Talbot, Rice D., *From Prehistory to the Thirteenth Century*. London: Thames & Hudson, 1967.

Tax, S., ed., *The Evolution of Man*. Chicago: University Press, 1960.

Taylor, G. R., *Sex in History*. London: Thames & Hudson, 1953.

Teilhard de Chardin, P., *Le Phénomène Humain*. Paris: Ed. du Seuil, 1955.

——, *Le Milieu Divin*. Paris: Ed. du Seuil, 1957.

The Cambridge Ancient History. Cambridge: University Press, 1970.

The Iliad of Homer and the Odyssey, Encyclopaedia Britannica (ed. R. M. Hutchins), 1952.

The Living Bible. London: Coverdale House, 1972.

Thomson, R., *The Psychology of Thinking*. London: Penguin, 1959.

Thorpe, W. H., *Learning and Instinct in Animals*. London: Methuen, 1963.

Thrasher, F. M., *A Study of 1,313 Gangs in Chicago*. Chicago: University Press, 1963.

Tiger, L., *Men in Groups*. New York: Random House, 1969.

Tinbergen, N., *The Study of Instinct*. Oxford: University Press, 1951.

———, *Social Behavior in Animals*. London: Chapman & Hall, 1973.

Toynbee, A., and others, *Man's Concern with Death*. London: Hodder & Stoughton, 1968.

Ucko, P., and Rosenfeld, A., *Paleolithic Cave Art*. London: World University Library, 1967.

Valentine, C. W., *The Psychology of Early Childhood*. London: Methuen, 1942.

Van Gennep, A., *La Formation des Légendes*. Paris: Flammarion, 1910.

Wach, J., *Sociologie de la Religion*. Paris: Payot, 1955.

Waddington, C. H., *The Ethical Animal*. London: Allen & Unwin, 1960.

Washburn, S. L., ed., *Social Life in Early Man*. London: Methuen, 1962.

Watson, L., *Supernature*. London: Hodder & Stoughton, 1973.

Webster, T. B. L., *Hellenistic Art*. London: Methuen, 1966.

———, *Everyday Life in Classical Athens*. London: Batsford, 1969.

Wells, H. G., *A Short History of the World*. London: Penguin, 1938.

———, *Mind at the End of Its Tether*. London: Heinemann, 1945.

Wendt, H., *The Sex Life of the Animals*, New York: Simon and Schuster, 1965.

Williams, L., *Man and Monkey*. London: Deutsch, 1967.

Winnicott, D. W., *The Child, the Family, and the Outside World*. London: Penguin, 1964.

Wolff, C. A., *A Psychology of Gesture*. London: Methuen, 1945.

Woolley, L., *The Beginning of Civilization*. New York: New American Library, 1965.

Young, J. Z., *An Introduction to the Study of Man*. Oxford: University Press, 1971.

Zeiner, F. E., *A History of Domesticated Animals*. London: Hutchinson, 1963.

Zuckerman, S., *The Social Life of Monkeys and Apes*. London: K. Paul, 1932.

Zweig, F., *Women's Life and Labour*. London: Gollancz, 1952.